The BAFFLER

VOLUME I   NUMBER 17

TABLE OF CONTENTS

We sent this issue to press in June 2006 from Ana Cruz's apartment high above the treetops in The Flamingo Hotel. As we watched cool wisps of mist drift inland from the lake, we wondered whether Ana's national team, Brazil, really was going to win the World Cup. Then we heard a voice, silky and reassuring, which seemed to come from the radio. "Paraguay," it said. The voice was familiar. We'd have sworn it was our old pal Matt Weiland. "It's all in my book," the voice continued. "Paraguay."

Well, we'll come right out and admit it. It's been some time since you've heard from us. The world has become a good deal more squalid and brutish in the couple of years since we fired off BAFFLER NO. 16. Sorry—we had no idea that would happen. But insofar as we have slacked in literary creation, we have made up for it in procreation. We've added three more mouths to the grasping welter of humanity, because that's what we're about at Team Baffler—the Culture of Life.

Meanwhile, work continues apace at the Experimental Station, our home on the South Side of Chicago. Some surly gentlemen from Indiana came to reclaim our trailer, forcing us to disperse our office appurtenances into numerous hidey-holes. Sometime this summer we'll move into our permanent home.

We would like to thank Gabriel Madeira for his hospitality. We would also like to thank Messrs. Tad Kepley, Jim Grauerholz, and Wayne Propst, all men of letters in the environs of Lawrence, Kansas, for sharing their historical recollections.

Tom Geoghegan's essay is excerpted with permission from the pamphlet "The Law in Shambles," published by the Prickly Paradigm Press (Chicago). Copyright © 2005 Thomas Geoghegan.

"The National Highway Defense Fund" is reprinted by arrangement with Viking, a member of Penguin Group (USA) Inc., from *The King of Kings County*, by Whitney Terrell. Copyright © 2005 Whitney Terrell.

Writers are invited to submit manuscripts, by mail only. Unsolicited poetry submissions won't be considered. Submissions without a self-addressed, stamped envelope will receive no response. We encourage essay writers to submit a one-page précis instead of the whole honking megillah.

Subscriptions to THE BAFFLER cost US$24 for four issues, post-paid, in the United States, and can be purchased by check at the address on this page. Credit card orders are taken at thebaffler.com and 1-888-387-8947.

The BAFFLER

P.O. BOX 378293
CHICAGO, ILLINOIS 60637
thebaffler.com

Publisher
Greg Lane

Associate Publisher
Emily Vogt

Editor
Thomas Frank

Managing Editor
Dave Mulcahey

Fiction Editor
Solveig Nelson

Poetry Editor
Jennifer Moxley

Associate Editors
George Hodak
Jim McNeill

Layout
Ana Cruz

Advertising Sales
Richard A. Grijalva

Founders
Thomas Frank
Keith White

THE GILDED MEAN

by Thomas Frank

I MOVED TO WASHINGTON, D.C., two and a half years ago, and every morning when I open up my newspaper this is what I see: congressmen purchased by lobbyists, illegal wiretapping, a war launched on false pretenses, a whole panoply of policies more or less openly designed to shift wealth upward. Sometimes these things make me angry. But as I make my way toward the editorial page of that same newspaper, I learn how unbecoming and wrongheaded my anger is. My attitude, it turns out, is part of a larger and much more serious problem: the dread disease of *partisanship*.

Indeed, for a certain segment of mainstream opinion—including the flagship "liberal" media concerns and the common run of Democratic strategists—each fresh Republican outrage seems to inspire not so much alarm as a new bout of self-examination. *Maybe we're missing a side to this story. Best not to appear out of touch. What do the polls say?* Lacking the inclination to challenge or fight, these paragons of polite opinion retreat to a soothingly righteous realm of fantasy they prefer to call *centrism*.

Exactly why the political opposition in this country still clings to the centrist ideal is a mystery. As a governing philosophy it seemed to work well enough for the Clintonites, whose triangulations and focus group soundings and sellouts of liberal causes enabled them to hold on to executive power. But as a strategy for the long term, centrism proved to be disastrous for the Democrats. As a philosophy of *opposition* it is manifestly unsound, even on its own simple geometric terms: You can't counterbalance the heavier side of a scale by jumping up and down on the fulcrum. Yet nothing seems to budge Washington's responsible non-Republican classes from their centrist fantasy. Why?

We can learn a bit about the mystery of centrism by watching how it captures the imaginations of the capital's typical new arrivals. Take a young, idealistic, politely liberal American, a recent graduate from one of our most exalted colleges, plunk this person down in Washington, I submit, and the ideological conclusions on which he or she will soon settle are as predictable as the falsetto ululations of next month's Britney Spears hit.

Partisanship, he or she will quickly learn, is the official taxonomical system of the capital, but it takes our golden youth just a few months to realize that this system is something of a fraud. Having issued everyone a "D" or an "R" on their first day in town, the system expects them to take part as the two political teams join battle at every level, from intern kegger to impeachment proceeding. On radio, TV, and especially the blogs, the heroes from each side can be seen, fighting day and night in a never-ending slugfest whose brutality is matched only by its pettiness. Blogger D heaps vicious put-downs on Blogger R for failing to find humor in a celebrated comedy routine. Blogger R blasts Blogger D for failing to show equal amounts of umbrage at a variety of outrages. The system is preposterous. It discredits itself almost automatically.

Spectators at Washington's slowly grinding defamation derby require only a short time to understand what a ghastly waste the whole thing is. Gang war is no way to run a government, our earnest newbie starts to think, let alone the most powerful government on the planet. Besides, the other side aren't demons. The red states aren't that different from the blue states. Putting a name on the problem, our youngster decides that what ails the nation is *polarization, extremism, faction*—the very peril that Madison warned against way back in Federalist 10.

Having arrived at this epiphany, our good neophyte looks around at the uniform niceness of the capital's middle-class zones and the thousands of high-achieving college graduates who are his colleagues—and who hail, just like him, from smiling, prosperous suburbs across the nation—and comes to the same set of conclusions arrived at by thousands of his predecessors. And thus is generated one of Washington's most persistent literary forms: the young person's passionate panegyric to centrism.

Politics, it occurs to these clear-eyed young believers, are just tragic. Politics are an old-folks' game long obsolete in this modern world. After all, it is obvious that extremes of left and right are wrong—a point that is usually nailed down merely by demonstrating that left and right exist, which in the capital is often sufficient proof by itself that the answer to all questions lies somewhere between. And it is just as obvious that right-thinking middle-class

people from good colleges all agree on the answers to the big problems. What is required, obviously, is bipartisanship. Better: a new bipartisanship. Even better: bipartisanship *with attitude*. Bold centrism. *Radical* centrism.

Thus does unthinking partisanship spawn unthinking consensus—consensus that nevertheless imagines itself as the *ne plus ultra* of wise, measured statesmanship. Space prevents me from describing the resulting body of work in all its annoying detail, but let me quickly enumerate some of its signal characteristics, aside from its mandatory bemoaning of partisanship:

- A gaping credulity for the fad ideas once associated with the "New Economy" and an abiding suspicion of New Deal social welfare programs, which are customarily dismissed as "industrial-age" or "Depression-era" relics.

- Political libertarianism, which for this particular class of people is so self-evident that it requires of its proponents not advocacy but simple assertion. (Of course free trade. Of course pro-choice. Fucking duh.)

- A writing style steeped in historical inevitability and a penchant for titles that include the word "Next."

And, lest I forget: shameless misappropriation of the phrase, *The Vital Center*. It comes as an eternally fresh surprise to each wave of brave young centrists when they discover that Arthur Schlesinger's famous 1949 book, which they worship because of its title, actually lays out a political program considerably to the left of their squishy sacks of policy goo. In fact, you can be almost certain that right now, at some dark martini bar in Logan Circle, a dejected young Phi Beta Kappan is feeling bummed after having just figured this out.

Then there is the bitter, grown-up version of the centrist creed, in which the same set of conclusions is arrived at by a different road. Now, instead of youthful idealism, centrism is the product of a callused lifetime of political observation—the only sensible stance remaining to someone who has attended a dozen national political conventions and watched a generation of politicians pretend to care about the folks of Iowa and New

Hampshire. While idealistic centrism tends to sprout from former Clinton speechwriters and the sort of think tanks that use the term "Generation X" in their mission statements, the hardened variety is strictly the stuff of major-league journalism. This is the centrism one finds, for example, on the DC blogs written by professional media types—*The Note*, run by ABC News, or *The Swamp*, maintained by the *Chicago Tribune*—where a superficial cynicism is de rigueur and everybody in the political news is a liar, a spinner, a sophist, and also (provided they aren't some horrid idealist) one of the gang.

The preeminent exponent of this variety of centrism is Joe Klein, the *Time* columnist who has written both a scalding fictional indictment of Bill Clinton the politician (*Primary Colors*, 1996) and an oily nonfictional celebration of Bill Clinton the president (*The Natural*, 2002). This might seem like a contradiction at first, but in fact Klein's earlier account of Clinton's rascality ultimately served to support his later conviction that Clintonism somehow embodied the authentic politics of the people—a "natural" politics, even—as opposed to the fancy schemes of intellectuals and ideologues.

Unfortunately, as Klein tells the story in *The Natural*, an "Era of Bad Feelings" deluged this born politician's career, drowned his naturalness in Xtreme partisanship. Clinton had his faults, but it was the idealists who really screwed things up, the righteous true believers who pulled both parties "to their respective extremes, where the most passionate advocates were festering." They fester, these unnaturals, but more damningly they *think*. Consider Klein's crowning put-down of the loathsome Newt Gingrich, which he quotes from Bob Dole: "This was a man"—Gingrich, that is—"with too many ideas." Klein might more accurately have chosen to describe Gingrich as a man with really bad ideas, or a man with fake ideas, or a man with effective ideas about how to do foolish things. But no. It is the *having* of ideas that offends, and thus the conflict is established: ideas (Newt) versus na-ture (Bill); insane partisanship versus the living, breathing, copulating flesh.

The *naturalness* of centrism is a common fantasy in this most unnatural of cities—in one column last year Klein even dubbed the collection of TV pundits and soft Ds who share his predictable politics as the "party of sanity." Even more to the point is the *New Republic*

> **It comes as an eternally fresh surprise to each wave of brave young centrists when they discover that *The Vital Center*, a book they worship because of its title, actually lays out a political program considerably to the left of their squishy sacks of policy goo.**

article of five years ago—still remembered fondly in Washington—which saluted conventional wisdom under the title, "Why What Everyone Thinks Is Usually Right." The reason it's right is because conventional wisdom is the end product of a "marketplace of ideas," see. And a market, as we all know, is a naturally occurring mechanism for delivering truth and quality, for ensuring that good things succeed while bad ones are filtered out. The conclusion is obvious: If the pundits aren't talking about something, it's because that something doesn't deserve to be talked about.

Which, as it happens, is pretty close to the way centrist Washingtonians tend to view themselves: as the cream of the meritocratic crop, the product of the great national marketplace in talent. They are here amid the cherry blossoms because they have been summoned here, by the same invisible, infallible hand of nature that earlier summoned them to Harvard or Stanford. They are here in middle-class paradise because they deserve to be here, and the political beliefs on which they all agree are, similarly, the most deserving of beliefs.

Lurking behind these assumptions is the "rational choice" strain of political science, a descendent of Chicago-school economics, with its reverence for markets and its perfectly calculating individual monads. The political version of *homo economicus* is known as the "median voter," and the superstition of market equilibrium here gives way to the rule of the all-powerful center, in which the exact middle of the opinion distribution is—magically but invariably—supposed to be the prevailing element in American politics. Just like moviegoers or car buyers, always forcing corporate America to deliver precisely the products the public craves, so the median voter is said to get exactly what he wants from politics. Which is to say, in effect, that he must have wanted whatever it is he happens to get.

Closely related is the doctrine of symmetry, in which non-centrists of left and right are, in their equally inexplicable manias, assumed to be precise mirror images of each other, culpable in every respect to precisely the same degree. If conservatives have been found guilty of some act of partisanship, then liberals must be guilty of some equivalent misdeed. If conservatives have "polarized" to the right, then liberals have "polarized" to the left. Since Jack Abramoff bribed Rs, the assumption goes, he must also have bribed Ds (an error in which the *Washington Post* once persisted, to its great regret). Washington journalism is so enslaved by this logic that it even extends to workaday movie reviews: A brief *Post* description of the documentary *Why We Fight* faulted the movie's director for criticizing conservative think tanks while not mentioning liberal ones, whose existence, presumably, levels the playing field. Sometimes centrist organizations suspend judgment altogether while they wait for left and right to balance out and reveal the true path, as in the case of the conservative *Post* blogger who got in trouble not because the *Post* determined that he was a plagiarist, but because he was *accused* of plagiarism by liberal bloggers, and then *was not defended* against the charge by conservative bloggers. In the *Post's* own account of the incident, the imbalance, not the plagiarism, was the decisive point. Woe betide him whom the bloggers will not defend.

~

Journalistic centrism seems ridiculous at times, but it is sweet reason when compared to the political centrism that has captured one of the nation's two major parties.

The two-party system is supposed to be the hardest of hard realities making centrism so natural and irresistible, but the two-party system is also what ensures that the consequences of a prolonged dalliance with centrism are dire if not fatal. Recall the exploits of the Democratic Party during the nineties, when its leadership turned ostentatiously away from its traditional faith. First, the party "triangulated" its core principles away, setting up a debilitating image problem that persists to this day. Then, having burned through its inherited beliefs, the party found that its traditional blocs of support, which were supposed to loyally balance the Rs while the leadership was boldly claiming the glorious center, had diminished with each clever sellout. Slowly but irresistibly, the party was dragged toward its opposite pole. The bridge to the twenty-first century was a bridge to nowhere. Better by far to choose the role of the party that doesn't compromise easily, that stands on principle and lets the other side seek the glorious center.

A less understandable error is the assumption, implicit in almost all centrist thinking, that the political landscape is an unchanging, statistically measurable mass of beliefs—"facts on the ground," the tough-minded *Note* likes to say—to which politicians must either conform or seek other employment. The centrists love to gaze tenderly upon the disillusioned political tough guy they see in the mirror, but for all their worldliness they have somehow managed to blink out one of the most basic facts of history: Politicians not only obey public opinion, they *make* public opinion. They can alter the "facts on the ground," they can build movements and change minds. The centrists' self-imposed ignorance of this is the reason they were caught napping by Ross Perot's crusade in 1992 and the trumped-up gay marriage panic of 2004. A zealous attentiveness to movement-building, persuasion, and mind-changing, on the other hand, is one of the reasons conservatives have enjoyed their improbable multi-decade winning streak. Mastery beats drift every time.

$\sim$

It is bracing and even a little shocking to turn from one's daily DC diet, with its gaseous reassurances of the middle-mind's wisdom, to a shot of reality like David Harvey's recent *Brief History of Neoliberalism*. This is not because Harvey is a startling or stylish writer—on the contrary, he is an academic geographer who chooses his words with care and is best known (at least by me) for making sense out of the last decade's scholarly wars over the nature of postmodernism. His new book achieves the effect it does through the simple device of speaking plainly about the momentous economic and political change that, beginning in the seventies, swept over America and then the rest of the industrialized world.

It is a story we all know instinctively, and it's not a very centrist affair. We have loosed the forces of the market, and this is what the market has done to the United States: It has destroyed manufacturing and enthroned finance; beaten organized labor almost to death; demanded round after round of tax cuts; defunded public services while raising the price of education and health care to inaccessible levels; decoupled wages from productivity, allowing wages to erode to a level lower today than in the early seventies despite all the advances in worker efficiency. We are often told that we live in a time of otherworldly prosperity, but what has changed the most, Harvey tells us, is distribution, not production. Our new economy is a banker's triumph, not an engineer's. Today the nation's affluent areas glitter, its blue-collar neighborhoods crumble, and its rich people are richer, as measured by their percentage of the national

income, than they have been since the twenties. The class divide has returned with a vengeance, with one class consistently getting what it wants while another just as consistently loses out.

This transformation ought to be the starting point for anyone writing about politics in America—or at least it ought to lurk some-

> **The centrists love to gaze tenderly upon the disillusioned political tough guy they see in the mirror, but for all their worldliness they forget that politicians not only obey public opinion, they make public opinion.**

where in the background of the discussion. It is the overarching story of our times, as much as industrialization was the story of the late nineteenth century and depression and war were the themes of our parents' generation. And yet the narrative as a whole, when Harvey puts it all together, has the feel of a secret history. This is partially a problem of terminology: The word that Harvey and others use to describe the age of markets, "neoliberalism," suggests to American ears more Michael Dukakis than Augusto Pinochet. It is also because our centrist rules of perception make the new order difficult to apprehend. Democratic presidents as well as Republicans pushed it along, making the free-market turn "bipartisan." Which is to say, *invisible*. According to the logic of journalistic centrism, there is no debate here. Instead, the prevailing custom among mainstream commentators is to view the deeds of the free market in the same category as acts of God or, better yet, as deeds of the sovereign People themselves.

In terms of everyday politics, however, the free market is anything but a democratic arrangement, a nice warm centrist choice that the folks in Ohio can feel good about. Almost wherever in the world you look, the road to the free-market order has been smoothed with brutally undemocratic machines. "Neoliberal theorists," Harvey writes, are "profoundly suspicious of democracy. Governance by majority rule is seen as a potential threat to individual rights and constitutional liberties." The people are supposed to be "free to choose," as in Milton Friedman's famous motto, but certain choices—labor unions, left-wing political parties—are off limits.

There has been nothing "natural" about it. In Chile and Argentina free-market reforms were implemented by military dictatorships, in Singapore by a one-party government, in China by a Communist regime. New York City drastically changed its fiscal policies in 1975 not because voters demanded it but because bankers did, as the price for resolving the city's bankruptcy crisis. Following this model, the IMF routinely demands (and receives) far-reaching policy changes from countries seeking its assistance. Free-trade agreements restrict government's ability to implement certain measures, while granting to businesses the power to relocate at will in their ceaseless search for the cheapest, most pliable labor force available. Pro-business policies are often made secretly (think of Dick Cheney's energy task force) or in little-scrutinized corners of government (tiny shifts in regulatory statutes bringing about massive shifts in regulatory practice).

Then there is the raw political power of organized money, subsidizing think tanks, authors, newspaper columnists, academics, magazines, and TV shows; funding the careers of friendly politicians and buying off dubious ones; and rewarding right-thinking regulators and bureaucrats when their stint in government is done. Indeed, as we have recently learned, the work of drafting legislation itself—especially the coveted "earmarks"—is sometimes simply a cash concession, much like the selling of papal indulgences in the Middle Ages. And as the business agenda is realized and the inequality worsens, the gravitational pull of money grows and grows.

What we do not learn from Harvey's global account are the precise mechanics of the change. Furnishing this detail is the business of Jacob Hacker and Paul Pierson, whose important new book, *Off Center*, is as devastating in its particulars as Harvey's account is in its grand theoretical terms. Here the scholarly framework is political science, and one finds little speculation about the connection between economics and culture, but the indictment zeroes in on the same point: An economic agenda that is essentially and inescapably unpopular has been fobbed off on the public. Hacker and Pierson set out to name and describe the procedure by which this has been accomplished, and in the process they have generated an invaluable field guide to the Republican Revolution.

The authors come to the battle armed with a simple yet potent little fact: Conservative economic policy is unpopular stuff. One might even say that, from tax cuts to Social Security privatization to last year's bankruptcy bill, it is *extremely* unpopular. Consider the big tax cuts of 2001, for example. "Public opinion was clearly and consistently hostile to the top-heavy skew of the Bush tax cuts," Hacker and Pierson write. "In fact, voters' leading concern about taxes . . . was that 'the rich pay too little in taxes.' " Now, of course, they pay even less.

To entertain such notions is inadmissible in the *bien pensant* circles of Washington journalism, where everything is as it should be and there can never be anything to be alarmed about. Hacker and Pierson, though, insist on the point. They swing it like a wrecking ball, using it to shatter all manner of illusions, both popular and scholarly. The center is supposed to hold the balance of power; it is supposed to get its way—and yet it has failed to do these things in recent years. Using their discipline's various methods for quantifying a politician's liberalism or conservatism, Hacker and Pierson demonstrate not only that today's Republican party is far to the right of where it used to be, but that it is moving more to the right all the time.

Despite it all the Republicans, as of this writing, control all three branches of government. Their control is razor-thin, yet they wield it like FDR—as if they were buoyed by a massive surge of popular adulation. How do they do it? How have they managed to stay on top?

The immediate answer is a dark form of political science in which the emphasis is on manipulating rather than obeying the legendary "median voter." Gerrymandering is the best-known weapon in this arsenal; Hacker and Pierson describe a bewildering welter of others. Republican leaders have learned how to control the political agenda, preventing troublesome matters from arising at all. They give measures deliberately misleading titles, knowing that the media will not bother to look beneath the surface until it's too late. They include time-bomb provisions in laws, forcing the hand of legislatures in the distant future, when public memory will have grown dim; they make tiny changes in regulatory policies where no one will notice until it's too late; they use boring old deficits to make funding crises unavoidable somewhere down the road. All of these are designed either to set up what Hacker and Pierson call "cognitive hurdles" or to "exploit limitations in voter knowledge."

It is, of course, customary in centrist-land to deny that "limitations in voter knowledge" even exist. Just as in free-market economics, good information is an assumption so fundamental to the theory that without it the entire edifice comes crashing down. Besides, the pseudo-populist response to any such assertion comes easily—so easily that you can hear it on Fox News every day: *You're saying the people are stupid!*

Yet the Republicans in Washington know that ignorance is real, and that it is structured by class. In a 2003 poll measuring people's attitudes toward taxes, recount Hacker and Pierson,

a majority of the richest 5 percent of Americans answered the knowledge questions correctly. Only a fifth of other Americans did, with knowledge lowest among the least affluent. Strikingly, only half of Americans even knew there had been a tax cut in 2001.

The wealthy, the Republican party's historical base, can be counted on to understand how

It is customary in centrist-land to deny that "limitations in voter knowledge" even exist. Yet the Republicans know that ignorance is real, and that it is structured by class.

well their servants have performed; those who have been screwed are, conveniently, the ones least likely to know it.

The book's larger and most consequential answer to the mystery of right-wing domination points to the large-scale changes in class power since the 1970s. We have all heard the libertarian argument that economic inequality is irrelevant—that it doesn't matter if we are heading toward a Gilded Age pattern of wealth distribution so long as we are all able to afford cars and TVs and pizzas and the other appurtenances of middle-class life.

Among the many mammoth facts such an argument overlooks are the *political* inequalities that economic inequality necessarily brings with it—and better information is only the first in a long list. The rich vote at higher rates than others, they contribute greater amounts to candidates, and, should they choose, they are able to afford today's expensive campaigns for public office. At the highest level, of course, they can also bankroll think tank operations charged with making their idiosyncratic personal ideas (such as Social Security privatization) into the common sense of the millions.

"Over the past thirty years, American politics has become more money-centered at exactly the same time that American society has grown more unequal," Hacker and Pierson write. "The resources and organizational heft of the well off and hyperconservative have exploded. But the organizational resources of middle-income Americans—from labor unions to mass-membership groups—have atrophied. The resulting inequality of resources and organization has not been neutral in its effects. It has greatly benefited the Republican Party while drawing it closer to its most affluent and extreme supporters."

~

Off Center is an important book; in fact, I think it is the most perceptive account of Republican Washington yet to appear. Hacker and Pierson have stretched the boundaries of their discipline to the very limit. But they do not break through.

When authors blast some prevailing theory as convincingly as Hacker and Pierson have done, they customarily abandon that theory and call on the world to adopt a new one. Hacker and Pierson demolish the cult of centrism, leaving no doubt that it has failed to account for the power of conservatism, that its doctrines of symmetry and polarization are little better than superstition—and yet they can never quite escape its clutches. For example, they never question the fundamental tenet of political geometry, in which proving that an idea is "off center" is enough to discredit it. Yet American history is crowded with lone geniuses and leaders whose views were unpopular at one time but who prevailed in the end—abolitionists, civil rights leaders, even the full-throated liberals of the early twentieth century. In fact, today's conservative activists identify themselves with such outcast visionaries so frequently that their claim on the mantle of the rebel is largely uncontested today. Angry with the world? Hate the powers that be? Meet George W. Bush, *Rebel-in-Chief* (the actual title of a recent book by Fred Barnes).

This failure to close the door on centrism leads Hacker and Pierson to a rather unfortunate moment. Having shown decisively that the "center" is not the all-powerful juggernaut its admirers describe, the authors suggest not that we abandon the theory, but that we change the nation's political structure in order to make the theory work—that we take steps to "make the votes of the middle more important," that we "empower moderate voters." In fairness, the specific measures that the authors go on to suggest are perfectly sensible, yet the reader is left wondering why the views of moderates should be privileged by the state, rather than the views of any other faction. Is it because moderates score four on some abstract scale of seven? Is this what democracy comes down to?

If we refuse to engage the contents of the ideas themselves, it unavoidably is. We are forced to conclude that the rule of the middle-mind is desirable because the rule of the middle-mind is the reigning fetish of political science. This is not democracy; it is professionalization run amok.

Far better to be done with the cult of the center for good. After all, it is not difficult to see how Washington's horror of strange ideas has drained our politics of interest and relevance and color and may therefore be responsible for the very voter apathy that centrists so love to lament. Maybe there's something to be said for the dreaded condition of "polarization"—maybe having politicians represent a broad range of opinions, rather than all of them clamoring after the same "median voter," is what a healthy "marketplace of ideas" ought to look like.

And while we're considering that, let's remember that the people who glory to call themselves "centrists" and "moderates," whether they are in journalism or politics, and whether they are young and idealistic or old and jaundiced, *aren't centrists at all.* On economic issues ranging from free trade to Social Security privatization (points of particular enthusiasm for arch centrists Thomas Friedman and Joe Klein, respectively) they stand well to the right of majority opinion. In their mystical adoration of markets and the magic of the New Economy—a veritable requirement of the pundit-licensing process, apparently, along with a mystical adoration of baseball—they are so far outside the main current of American opinion that they might as well be on the moon. The only "center" these people occupy is a kind of middling position in the range of views commonly expressed in the management suites of the nation's office buildings. What they deserve to be a subject of is not poli-sci reverence but searching sociological examination.

The political solution, then, is not to rig the game so that we might once again enjoy the rule of some triangulating Democrat who can proceed to get a Social Security deal done. It is to build a force that will counter the free-market ideology of the right—and also of the "center"—not merely by pointing out that it is unpopular, but that it is thunderingly wrong. ∎

THE RULE OF LAW IN SHAMBLES

by Thomas Geoghegan

Being a labor lawyer, and blinkered anyway by one or two big ideas, I tend to look at things the way a labor economist does. So when I wonder about the countless aspects of American public life that are falling apart, I always come back to the same explanation: It's because of the low-and-falling hourly wage. For example: Why do we have growing mass poverty in the U.S.? Because we have more people working at a low-and-falling hourly wage. Why crime and drugs? More people working at a low-and-falling hourly wage. Why do kids drop out of school? Because their families work for a low-and-falling hourly wage. Why do people stop voting and give up on public life? They see no hope, they're overwhelmed, and so on—but the ultimate reason for it is that more and more of them are working at a low-and-falling hourly wage.

It's falling in absolute terms, due to loss of health insurance and pensions. It's falling in real terms, adjusted for inflation. It's falling in relative terms, by which I mean relative to what the millions of us who are rich and super-rich can buy.

So while each book I have written has its own privileged big fact, there is really but one Big Fact that loops in and out of everything I write: the unfairness of it all, over the last thirty years or more. How most of us get less and less per hour. Even as the country as a whole gets more and more.

As this inequality has worsened, I have seen, in my own life, big changes in the legal system. We may still be equal before the law—for now. Maybe. It's arguable. But even if it's true for now, how much longer can it last? As inequality gets worse, our super-rich, even if undertaxed, will eventually pay the bulk of the taxes. And they will ask, *Why pay for a rule of law that applies to all of us equally?*

I can't even use a word like "us" to describe the country now. In an essay I read a few months ago, Yale economist Robert Shiller estimated that the bottom 40 percent of American families, by income, used to account for 18 percent of all national income. It's now under 14 percent and going south—soon it will be under 10 percent. These numbers may not shock you so much, but think about it: Close to half the country will end up with about one-tenth of the income, and virtually none of the wealth. In all the history of all time I know of no case in which a country with so much inequality was able to sustain for long any real kind of democratic self-government.

Instead, we get a kind of plutocracy. The top 1 percent already have 16 percent of the income—which is more than the bottom 40 percent put together. Before long the top 1 percent will have more income than half the population—i.e., more than a whole majority, the majority that arguably should but can't elect a Democrat.

A plutocracy like this teaches people in many subtle ways to be servile. There are few unions, of course. No one dares to ask for more. People learn to bow and scrape. And they also learn to withdraw, to drop out, to disengage.

Plutocracy also destroys the moral character we need for any stable rule of law. The rich naturally feel less and less responsibility for the rest of us. But it's the middle class that worries me most. There is good reason

13

to think the middle class is becoming corrupt as well.

"Corrupt?" Yes. Consider this single fact: It took ten years, almost all of the nineties, for the median family income to get back to the same level that it was, in real terms, in 1989. But in 1999, when we got to the same income level we had in 1989, this same "median" family had to work . . . *six more weeks a year.*

To keep from falling, our middle class had to work, for free, six more weeks a year. Not a few more hours: *six more weeks!* (By the way, maybe it's worth pausing to say: No wonder our GDP keeps shooting up, what with so many people working for free.) And all this unpaid extra labor tends to undermine the rule of law.

Why? The economist John Maynard Keynes put it best: "Nothing corrupts a society more," he wrote, "than to disconnect effort and reward." That's what did in the old Soviet Union: No matter how hard people worked, they could not get ahead of those who did not work at all. And that is what is happening in America too. In a certain way, of course, our country is the very opposite of the old Soviet Union. Here, if people don't work, they're going to end up being homeless. Though if they do work, they may still end up being homeless. And all the while, they hear about dot-com riches and stock-market winnings being showered on people who haven't really done much of anything.

That's the point. Like in the USSR, we too are slowly breaking the connection between effort and reward. And so people in the middle start to see the world as arbitrary and unfair; it is unpredictable, a matter of luck, with a chance of catastrophe around the corner. It does not matter if they work the extra hours: More than 40 percent of American families have less than $5,000 in savings. One bill, out of the blue, can blow everything away.

So, quietly and to themselves, people start to wonder, as the country becomes fabulously wealthy: *Why play by the rules?*

I may even understate the case. The disconnect between effort and reward is actually

much greater than it seems from the figures that I gave above. Many people really did not get back to the "same 1989 level of income" in 1999. Think of pensions. Fewer people had them. Think of health insurance. Fewer people had it. Perhaps our moral character can survive one decade of that kind of thing. But it keeps going on.

Why is this so dangerous for the rule of law? It's simple, I think. If we do not expect the world to be reasonable and fair, then sooner or later we do not demand or expect it from the law. We get used to the arbitrary and the unfair. Sometimes we take a certain glee in it, at least when it happens to others.

But in our own lives we experience it as alien. We did not consent to it. We did not vote for it. And so, in a plutocracy, we don't trust the government. Why should we? It does nothing for us, it is underfunded, and it's unreliable.

This attitude, in turn, makes the problem worse. The more arbitrary and unfair we think things are, the more we drop out. We don't simply stop voting. We stop reading the paper. Stop following it at all.

And the more we drop out, the more arbitrary and unfair the rule of law does indeed become. It is not just that people now *perceive* the law as less rational and predictable. It really is.

Here is how it is becoming less rational and predictable. The longer I practice law, the more it seems the law is turning into "tort." What I liked in law school was "contract" law, where we studied written agreements in rational, objective ways. Tort is different: It is an "injury to my person." It is a punch in the eye, it is a libel to my good name, it is something for which I go to court for damages, in maybe a tiny or maybe a big amount.

As a labor lawyer, I see little or no contract law anymore because the unions have collapsed. All we have now are suits for violations of civil rights, for an "injury to my person." It's not the union that goes to an arbitration on my behalf—it's me, the injured party, who gets a lawyer and goes screaming into court for damages.

And as with contract, so with administrative law, the defense of the public by a neutral civil service. Where the government used to take care of us, now we are on our own. As the state collapses and becomes more arbitrary in its enforcement of the law, all of us are more in need of tort (i.e., "trial") lawyers.

I slipped into law school as the New Deal consensus was falling apart. Deregulation had begun. And soon, instead of the administrative law or the contract law of the old regulatory state, we had tort law or private law. Today it is the trial lawyers who do what civil servants used to do. Why? Because after 1972 we began wave after wave of deregulation, dismantling not just economic regulation but even public safety: worker safety, food safety, transportation safety.

Some may object: "Wait, I don't think we deregulated everything! Maybe we deregulated energy. Maybe we deregulated telecoms. What do you mean, we deregulated *safety?*"

I know: more liberal hysteria. Okay, I am hysterical about it.

It did not always happen formally. Sometimes it just happened when regulatory agencies were defunded. Remember the teaching of the great law professor Clyde Summers: "It costs a lot of money for people to have 'rights.' "

Think of the deficits under Reagan. Now under Bush. Those ascending deficits tracked the degree of our deviation from the rule of law. Not because those big, scary numbers ever threatened any shortfall in entitlements —legally, none can occur. What deficits triggered, and continue to trigger, is the slow weakening of the *execution* of the laws. Deficits morph almost automatically into cuts in discretionary spending, especially for lawyers, regulators, and administrative judges.

> **With the gutting of the regulatory state, we have replaced the civil servant with the whistleblower and the trial lawyer. Instead of the rule of law we have tiny acts of martyrdom and rage.**

Not to mention the inspectors of workplace safety, food safety, automobile safety, drug safety—safety pure and simple.

Because we regard the rule of law as if it were a free lunch—as if it costs nothing to execute the laws—we fail to grasp what the numbers have to tell us. In a single year it's hard to see. But every year, Congress cuts a little more out of the "discretionary" budget. Fewer people. Less money. And now to make sure the civil servants don't even ask for money, Congress has started to prohibit unions in agencies such as Homeland Security. The effect is the same: Government does less. And talented people are scared off from public service. Of course, with today's whopping student loans, those who used to go into public service would have to stay out now anyway. We have lost a whole generation of talented people in this way, and now the government itself seems more inept than ever.

Yes, it's hard to see it. But let me give a small example. During the last Bush-Kerry debate, the CBS man asked, "What about the shortage of vaccine for the flu?" Bush could only mumble. Kerry ducked it, too. He talked instead about his plan for health insurance. But I wish Kerry had said: "Yeah, the government screwed it up. What do you expect? We don't get good people in the government anymore. And the ones we do have are overworked. Look, if we don't want to pay to have a decent civil service—and, by the way, decent law enforcement—this is what we're going to get."

And as we keep gutting the public sector, we'll see panics like this more and more.

In my practice, I see over and over again the evils of the deregulation of safety. If someone like me can see these evils—and I do barely any administrative law—they must be epidemic. Let me pick a few:

Work. The Labor Department, which I know best, seems to me the saddest case. I could pick any office, OSHA, or ERISA. But let's take the poor, overwhelmed Wage and Hour Division of the Labor Department. All across the country, people at Wal-Mart have been working off the clock—for free. And God knows what is happening in the back rooms at the smaller places. No one knows.

There's no one in the field to investigate.

It's private lawyers who bring minimum-wage lawsuits today, not government. Yet we lawyers can't even find the worst cases. I mean the people who are in slavery. Some of it white slavery. Oh, sure, someone occasionally escapes from a cellar, and it ends up in the *New York Times.* I know a reporter who's got enough to write a book. Indeed, he's writing it now. But why can't the government find them? Same answer: There's no one in the field.

Once I filed a suit to get the Labor Department to enforce the child labor laws for sixteen- and seventeen-year-olds, kids whom they do not even pretend to protect. I got nowhere. I met with a Labor Department lawyer who told me: "Look, suppose I say I agree with you. How would I ever get the money to enforce it?"

He was right. If I had won and they had issued regulations, it would only have been worse. In the Labor Department, as in agency after agency, there is a vast, complex body of regulatory law that no one now enforces. Yes,

the law is "there." On paper. Indeed, it is on a *lot* of paper. Fifty paperback volumes, in total: I know because I counted. But for big chunks of these volumes, there's no one to enforce it.

So that leaves it to the private sector, to ordinary citizens, to figure out some way to enforce the law by themselves. We can't look to civil servants. Instead we look to vigilantes. In particular, we look to trial lawyers, who cherry-pick the good cases—i.e., those where they stand to make a pile. Or in the case of many Labor Department regulations, we look to the working poor, to our maids and parking valets who, we hope, will one day decide to blow the whistle. Scream. Do something. Even if they're fired. What's replaced the civil servant? The whistleblower. Instead of the rule of law, we now have these tiny acts of martyrdom and rage.

Here's another area of law where I see it more and more.

Health. Or let's say *patient safety.* Since I represent nurses, I can see, in this one area, how the rule of law is in shambles.

The hospitals everywhere are cutting back on nurses. That's how they drive up profit margins. The ratio of nurses to patients is ballooning. Patients sit for hours in emergency rooms. It takes longer to start the orders. Oh, sure, there are a lot of regulations telling the hospitals what to do. But there aren't enough nurses to carry them out.

Or civil servants to enforce them.

Who knows? Maybe there aren't enough trial lawyers to bring the medical malpractice cases!

At any rate, it galls me to hear the president complain about trial lawyers suing hos-

pitals. Why is it, he should ask his advisers, that the trial lawyers happen to bring all these suits? It's because the hospitals depart from a standard of care, often set out in federal regulations, which the president of the United States himself has the duty to enforce. And why do the hospitals depart from those standards of care?

Not enough inspectors.

Not enough nurses on the floor.

If the president really wanted to cripple the hated trial lawyers, he might consider, as a starter, setting nurse-to-patient ratios. Of course he won't. Yet as hospitals cut back on nurses, they end up violating more standards and regulations.

Result? More and more patients die. Bring on the trial lawyers! When the rule of law really is in shambles, that's what people get. When we have no contract, we get more suits in tort. And when we deregulate, we get more torts as well. One can measure the rise of tort law from the drop in the numbers of those who simply watch over us. I mean not only the civil servants but the nurses on the hospital floor.

With the decline in administrative law, I have become a kind of trial lawyer, too. Or at least I file suits for whistleblowers—that is, suits for the "tort" of wrongful discharge. I think of P, a nurse who works at Hospital Q. Or she did until the hospital fired her. She was a red-hot pepper of a whistleblower. She fired up the nurses. She urged them to file "assignment-despite-objection forms" by the dozens. *I am working under protest because there aren't enough nurses to cover patients.* All over the state of Illinois, she set up hearings for a Patient Safety Act. And she sent off petitions to get state officials to come look at conditions at the hospital.

Which at last they did.

In other words, she is working for us, the public, like a private attorney general. She is doing it without pay—and soon without her job.

When the hospital fired her, I filed suit. Oh, the hospital hates her, calls her a liar, and threatens to sue her for libel. And, sure, a battle like this is fun sometimes, at least for a few moments. Example: her deposition. It went on all day. I had a little fun, seeing the way the hospital lawyer dished it out to her, and then seeing the way she dished it right back. Both were very good. Yes, at moments, I enjoy an eight-hour deposition.

Otherwise, it was just another day in hell.

In any event, this is what passes for the rule

How bad have things gotten? I am now in a legal battle where we have to prove that the Department of Agriculture ever bothers to enforce the law at all.

of law in America today. It's as if a nurse has to pour gasoline over herself and strike a match in order to get the attention of a public health official. But there is another area that is even worse.

Safety. Like meat inspection. How could regulation possibly be collapsing here, with all the worries about hormones and mad cow disease? Well, it is.

I am now in a legal battle where we have to prove that the Department of Agriculture *ever bothers to enforce the law at all.*

Sound surreal? It is. The suit is with the owner of a chicken-processing plant. We are suing for his workers under the so-called WARN Act, which requires that a plant issue a notice before closing. In this case, the plant owner did not give the required sixty days of notice before he closed. "But the Department of Agriculture shut me down," the owner argued. "How could I foresee that?" He argued that yes, he may have done bad things, and let rats run wild, and also let those rats shit on the chicken meat. And, yes, it is even true that the Agriculture Department inspectors gave him "write ups."

But here is the issue: Was it reasonable for the owner to foresee that the USDA would enforce its own regulations?

His argument was this: "I am in the business, and they never enforce the law." Never. That was his claim: The Department of Agriculture is more or less a joke. Under Bush I, then Clinton, and then Bush II, it's gotten worse. "Everyone knows!" Now comes the ruling of the district judge, who is a liberal, a Clinton appointee: Yes, he says, it *was* unforeseeable. It was as if he took judicial notice that, as a matter of common knowledge, *the government does not enforce the laws.*

Case dismissed!

I'm still in shock that the employer got away with such an argument. Yet he had a point.

We really did cut back on inspectors. We really don't impose fines. So he had no way of knowing the USDA would actually shut him down.

In other words, the application of the rule of law is the equivalent of an "act of God." Like a hurricane.

Yes, we appealed. I helped edit the brief. (It was my colleague's case.) All I did was to strike out the word "rodent" and put in the word "rat." And the word "rat" came up a lot: The plant was filthy, full of rats and rat droppings, all over the meat. The scary part was that the plant had gone on like this for years. The more we deregulate, and the more the inspectors are told not to threaten but to "cooperate" and to show a "cooperative spirit," the more the rodents, or the rats, are free to go on dropping on our take-out fried chicken.

So what happened on appeal? Well, of course we argued that a judge cannot assume that it is "unforeseeable" for the laws ever to be enforced. In America, has the rule of law really come to that? Even though we got the district court reversed, we did not really win the point.

No. We have to go to trial.

We have to have a trial as to whether or not the owner of the chicken plant should *believe* the government when it says to him,

We're going to enforce the law.

Again, it's not just patient safety or food safety—it's any kind of safety. Lately I have been representing locomotive engineers, and it's even true of rail safety. Rail safety! People are dying. There are terrible accidents. But what do we do? We cut the number of inspectors. Last November, the *New York Times* ran two front-page stories on how the Federal Railroad Administration is going easy on Union Pacific. Let's be nicer even as the accidents get worse.

And, of course, we have whistleblowers here too. I mean literally—the engineers. But they can only blow the whistle if they have a strong union and can keep their federal licenses. But as I write this, Union Pacific is trying to take away the licenses of some of them without the due process federal regulations require.

As long as the FRA goes easy on Union Pacific, this will be a tough battle for those engineers. And if the union does not win, then be careful when you cross the tracks.

Rail safety, for God's sakes! How nice if this were just a case of the New Deal in shambles. But now it's a case of the *Square Deal* in shambles. I mean, the regulatory state as it existed under Theodore—not Franklin—Roosevelt. Sure, I'd like to curb the trial lawyers, as would our president. I, too, hate to see the law turn into tort. But without the trial lawyers, I might be dead. A train wreck. A spill of deadly gas.

Where I live, in Chicago, I'm in a ring of nuclear power plants. I'd be in terrible danger if we ever successfully muzzled the trial lawyers. It's only the tort system that saves us from another Three Mile Island. Yes, I agree, it might be nice if we had more nuclear plants. We could cut down on Mideast oil. We could slow down global warming. And if I lived in France, with all its nuclear energy, I might think it was a good thing. So why do I oppose it here?

Because France has a real administrative state, a real civil service, and the best and brightest do the regulating. In America, we can't even keep the trains on the tracks. And so, sure, as a citizen, I'd like to curb the trial lawyers.

But I also want to live.

You may well scoff at the specter of another Three Mile Island, or a Bhopal, or even, God forbid, a Chernobyl here in the U.S. And if we suppressed the trial lawyers maybe we'd get lucky and none of that stuff would ever happen. But consider what happened in one case where we did put the lid on trial lawyers.

Corporate finance. Enron. WorldCom. How did it happen? We got rid of administrative law and then we got rid of tort law. Then the whole thing blew up. Here is how I tried to explain it one day at lunch to a lawyer friend, Mary M.

"First, in Stage One: we had the SEC, the Securities and Exchange Commission. The New Deal. Joe Kennedy. We got the best, the brightest. We regulated like hell.

"Then in Stage Two, we got deregulation. We cut back enforcement. Instead of the New Deal, we got New Deal Lite.

"Then there's Stage Three. In come the trial lawyers. With Reagan they move in. They start to file a lot of class actions, for non-disclosure and fraud. The corporate people say: Stop it!

"So fine, Stage Four, we stopped it. We got the Contract with America, Newt Gingrich, the Republican Congress. They passed a lot of laws. We zapped a lot of suits. Corporate people were happy.

"So then, Stage Five: *ka-boom.* Enron. World-Com. It's Chernobyl. Everything blows up.

"So now, in Stage Six, we have Sarbanes-Oxley. We make the CEOs sign balance sheets with statements reading, 'I do not engage in fraud.' But is that Mickey Mouse? Yeah. So what is it we really do?

"We turn it over to Eliot Spitzer, the attorney general of New York. A state attorney general, even if the state is New York. He sues the banks, the big companies. The leading regulator of not just the American but the *world* economy is now the *state attorney general of* New York. I like Eliot Spitzer. I do. Thank God for him.

"But the attorney general of one state? Every three or four years we have a new legal paradigm. We get the SEC, then tort, then laissez-faire, then self-regulation, and then a state attorney general. It's all in shambles."

Mary M listened quietly, and then she said: "It's like a boiler, isn't it? You try to get rid of the pressure in one place, and it blows up

What sets payday loan stores apart from the Mafia is that the state of Illinois is working as a kind of "silent partner."

somewhere else."

We got rid of the New Deal, the old administrative law, and now we're about to get rid of torts. Guess what's going to happen? The boiler's going to blow.

Mary's right. What happened at Enron or WorldCom is just as likely to happen in the emergency room or at a Kentucky Fried Chicken or on a rotting railroad track. I hate the way the law is melting into tort, but I'd rather have a trial lawyer than nothing at all.

If the breakdowns in patient safety, or food safety, or rail safety do not convince you that the regulatory state is now in shambles, and if the legal anarchy in corporate finance is not enough to do it either, then I ask you to consider one final case.

Payday loans. With the payday loan stores, we have gone from administrative law to no law. We have hit the bottom. No rule of law at all.

I got involved in a suit against payday loans; otherwise, I would no more have noticed them than I notice Taco Bells. Except for the late Monsignor John J. Egan, old civil rights hero, friend of Saul Alinsky. Before he died, he dragged me onto a committee to investigate payday loans. I even ended up filing a suit, which turned out to be mainly a *cri de coeur.* (I mean, we lost.) But let me tell you what a payday loan is, and why it is such an apt symbol of the collapse of regulation.

Let's say I'm making $30,000 a year, I have a family, and I'm short two hundred bucks this month. I go to you, Mr. Payday Loan, at one of your convenient offices found on just about any street corner in Chicago. Now, of course, I don't literally turn over my next paycheck. But in return for $200, I write you a postdated check for $240.

I know, you know, and the state of Illinois knows that at the moment I write that check, it is almost certainly a bad check. It may be "postdated," but under the law these days, that means nothing. My bank is allowed to cash it now, right away, as soon as I write it. And we both know that I don't have enough in my account to cover it. That's why I've come to you.

So right away, I have set myself up. Because if you cash it, and it bounces, I'm in big legal trouble. Maybe I'll be prosecuted. And the risk of it grows if I can't come up with the money next month. So to avoid the prosecution, or some other legal trouble, I now roll it over for an even bigger loan.

And another.

And another.

I keep writing bad checks, and I keep giving you more and more power to put me into jail. Soon I can owe a thousand dollars for a loan of just two hundred. Even the Mob hesitates, I believe, to overreach like that.

Yet I have to admit that, at the beginning, I was annoyed with Father Egan for dragging me into these meetings and paying so much attention to this one little issue of payday loans. Come on! This was a priest who had marched for civil rights. He was a kind of sixties hero. Aren't there bigger things to take on than these stupid payday loans? But it slowly dawned on me what was so awful about the damned things.

What sets payday loan stores apart from the Mafia is that the state of Illinois is working as a kind of "silent partner." I mean, the state sets up and licenses every lender: "We the state know exactly what you're doing. We the state know that you are inducing people to write you a bunch of bad checks. And when you give us the word, we the state will throw these suckers into jail." In other words, the state is part of the scam; it helps induce the poor to commit a crime, and it acts as enforcer should they step out of line. In effect, it is setting up America's penniless for prosecution.

What's more, the state's involvement is essential to the operation because otherwise the payday loan store is subject to a cap. Yes, in the old days, before deregulation, there was a cap on interest. Technically, it still exists in Illinois. In theory, the cap on interest here is 9 percent. But this 9 percent cap applies to nothing. No state in our union could enforce that kind of cap. The global banks laugh at single digits. They charge you and me—on our VISAs—double digits. And the hapless poor, they want to charge them triple digits.

True, in some places there is a limit on the exploitation of the poor. But not in Illinois. And Illinois is one of the better states. It's a blue state. It's liberal. It has a liberal Democratic governor. It has a Democratic state house and state senate. And yet the state is essential to the scam.

As I write this, Father Egan's group has gotten at least some limit on the ability of the lenders to keep rolling over the loans. But the payday loan industry is still going to thrive at interest rates that our ancestors would have been shocked to pay.

So in Illinois, after much effort we have modestly regulated usury. And will that help matters in the end? It may be that "reform" ends up sanctioning the overcharge. So while on the surface we seem to gain a bit more public trust, we will end up ultimately with much more private rage.

Father Egan, you were right. Payday loans may not be the worst thing. But they're a perfect metaphor for the collapse of the New Deal. Why shouldn't people experience government as arbitrary and unfair, when many of our states are still too weak to cap interest at even 200 percent?

And so they forget about the state doing anything to stop the fall of the hourly wage. It is certain to go on falling for at least another thirty years.

Meanwhile, as we live in fear of being sued by debt collectors whom the government cannot control, more of us feel justified in filing any suit we can. Student loans, payday loans, medical bills: America is suing us, and we are suing America back. It's all against all. Life is unfair. But then so is the law.

And as more of us withdraw from civic life, it only gets worse.

What to do? Well, you can go out and be a whistleblower and file your own suit. Are we blowing whistles or just blowing off steam? They say that in India the authorities like to see more people sue. Better they blow off steam by going into court than by going out in the street and organizing the poor.

Yes, I know the objection. I raise it myself: We have to work through the political system, and build a majority. Believe me, I am appalled that even in presidential elections barely half the electorate votes. Yes, of course, we must use the political system. But it's not one or the other. We have to blow the whistles, too. Indeed, we have to beat the drums. And sound the tocsins. ■

WILLIAM BURROUGHS

MY PART IN HIS DOWNFALL

by *Andrew O'Hagan*

IT WAS A SAVAGE SUMMER for famous writers. They were either being rolled by their former wives, dissed by their former publishers, or busy getting dead in the heat of Kansas. We had seen this kind of thing before: F. Scott Fitzgerald never went to Kansas, but Zelda was the roller-in-chief; the closest Hemingway got was Kansas City, where he learned to write and dreamed of being the youngest person ever to die. But believe me, the summer I'm talking about saw hot war break out between one kind of self-consciousness and another: Our minds were light and our hearts were dark in that August of 1997, those perfect weeks, that restless year, before Bill got impeached and Diana died.

I was in New York (writing and presenting a documentary film about Jack Kerouac) and I'd just found a large bloodstain on the carpet of Room 611 of the Gramercy Park Hotel. Never mind, I told myself, this is America, the maid is no doubt from a despotic country and will know what to do. So I put on a clean white T-shirt, stonewashed jeans, and spread cherry lip balm on my Scottish lips: It's best to be prepared for sex in New York, not because you expect any but because people don't trust you in New York if you don't look as if you're ready for sex at any time. I got in a taxi and went to see Adele Mailer. She looked like a cool Hispanic granny with a handbag and an unforgiving eye. "I've just come from the Actors Studio," she said, and immediately I thought of Kim Stanley doing *Bus Stop* to a crowd of fully famous students and note-takers and Strasbergs. Adele had written a book about being married to Norman Mailer and she kept using the letters "O.J." to describe

her relationship with him, or, more accurately, her relation to the incident in 1960 when Norman stabbed her with a kitchen knife during one of their parties. I asked Adele if she felt better now that she'd written the book. "I'll feel better when the money starts coming in," she said. Then she started talking about her old flame Jack Kerouac and the Greenwich Village scene of the 1950s. "Jack," she said, "was lousy in bed." Then she said Kerouac didn't like the taste of a certain spermicidal cream, a detail I've never quite forgotten, and then she said he wasn't enough of a man for her. She added that Allen Ginsberg once told her that if he ever went straight she would be the woman for him. "Oh, Adele," I said, "I bet he said that to all the girls."

Robert Giroux was sitting in a sort of wooden throne at the American Arts Club. A lovely old man with a plume of white hair, I thought he showed the accumulated wisdom of a life spent getting the commas right, publishing Eliot and Lowell, and not giving up on the little things. He sat with a watery-eyed old-timer and a young editor from Farrar, Straus called Ethan. Giroux told me a story, off-camera, about Djuna Barnes and James Laughlin, the founder of New Directions. He said that Barnes was complaining about the lack of royalties from that novel of hers—what is it, *Nightwood*? "Anyway, she complained to Laughlin, and the publisher said to her that he had been taught at his mother's knee to be a truthful person, and he had not held back a single penny from Djuna on her book. She went away. The next day Laughlin was walking down the street when he saw Barnes coming toward him. She came right up to him and stopped: "How's your mother's knee?" she asked. Giroux's friend then told how when Ezra Pound was stuck in St. Elizabeth's Hospital, some visitor asked him what he had thought of Djuna Barnes. He sat thinking for a long time. "Well," he said finally, "she ain't cuddly!"

When I got to Lowell, Massachusetts, John Sampas was already waiting. He smoked long cigarettes and wore sunshades inside and out, like Hunter S. Thompson, which made you think he might be a little impressed with his current job running the Kerouac estate. The house used to be owned by an old lady who was the first person in the town to own a telephone. Her number was 4. Sampas said her ghost still comes rattling from room to room, nowhere to go. His sister Stella married Kerouac late in his life, and when Kerouac died she inherited everything, including his sick and controversial mother. That morning, Sampas had gone to the local bank to get some manuscripts (that's where he stores them) and he showed them to me in the sitting room. One of them was just a note scribbled on the back of an envelope—Kerouac telling a friend he had gone out to play football.

When we were standing outside the Lowell high school a guy came up to talk. He had known Kerouac. The guy's brother had been a star athlete—the street we stood on, Koumanzalis, was named after his brother. The guy spoke of a mad trip he had made with Kerouac down to New York one time. He said they were drunk and high the whole week; then there was "the black thing." We asked him what he meant. He said that Kerouac

was always getting into fights with black guys; he'd insult them or argue with them in bars and sometimes he'd get beaten up. Koumanzalis said he thought this was what got Kerouac killed in the end, down there in Florida in 1969. He said he thought a couple of those young rednecks Kerouac was hanging out with would have got him beaten up good and proper. He remembered Jack phoning him a few days before he died. He said he had gotten licked in a bar, and he couldn't remember much, but he knew that his stomach was sore and that the whole of life was bad as hell. When I spoke to Carolyn Cassady (the wife of Kerouac's hero, Neal), she said Kerouac had stopped being a writer when it came to those late-night calls. "It was too sad," she said. "Just filth. That's all he spoke."

People are always asking me nowadays what the essential difference is between fiction and non-fiction, and I'm now ready to give a full and frank answer: In fiction, nothing is made up. There's a truth at the end of every line and, sometimes too, in the curve and weight of every word. At the end of every line of reportage or memoir—if it's any good—a doubt is raised and a question is left unanswered: Was it really like that? With good fiction we are never inclined to ask if it was really like that. Now, take this piece you are reading. If it was a short story, as many of you may imagine it to be—a tale rolled out by a fictioner, conjured on a group of days from the ambitious heart of some new voice in American fiction—would the piece you are reading satisfy you less, or more? If all of this was confected—Adele Mailer, the Gramercy Park Hotel, Scottish, Ezra Pound—would you feel cheated, or flattered? When I tell you that the speaker in this piece of memoir is real, that the events described here actually happened, are these useful or necessary pieces of information? Do they add anything? Let me tell you this is a problem not only for readers. Writers, too, begin to doubt their own relation to reality—and, for many of us, our talent begins its life with such doubtings. The summer I've described to you happened.

It happened in the order I've described and included the spoken words I've given you.

The next and decisive part of the narrative involves my arrival in Kansas. I realized, when I started writing this, that I'd told the story so many times in so many bars that it might be worth checking that I hadn't in fact made it up in the first place. My checks have proved decisive and gripping: I didn't make the story up, but I have changed the story again and again in small ways over time. My journal entries from 1997 tell a more serious and alarmed story; my gleeful renderings of the narrative since then have added historical weight to the soul of the piece, as well as numerous comedy touches, more personal involvement, further absurdity, and the renowned literary agent Andrew Wylie. The story of the story is not better than the story itself, just truer, whatever that means, and it has the virtue of taking us further into the realm where the question of reliability provides its own theatrical narrative.

Lawrence, Kansas, on a hot day. After it was all over, when I first told the story back in London, I'm sure I said it was the hottest day since records began. There is no evidence for that—it was just a very hot day. I arrived with a BBC television crew at a motel on the outskirts of Lawrence that had no food except donuts. At the Brisbane Writers Festival two years ago, I'm sure I said no food except chewing gum, and at a comedy festival that took place in a boat on the River Thames, I said it had no food except boiled soap and bath towels. We were in Lawrence to interview the novelist William Burroughs. When I told the story during the Democratic National Convention in Boston (to the editor of this journal), it was quite late at night: We were in J.J. Foley's Bar and Grill (or maybe the bar before that) and I told my interlocutors that I had spoken to William Burroughs several times before the interview was to take place in Lawrence. This has always been a crucial part of the story. It always gets sighs and laughs. "Kerouac's mother was a witch," I drawl. "She made him drink. And she drank herself," I say, quoting what Burroughs said to me.

"Don't say much more," I said to him, "because I want you to be fresh for the cameras tomorrow."

Now, despite being asked by everybody, I've never written the story you're reading until now. I always said I was keeping it for something, but now I realize the reason I held back is because I thought I might per-

No one anymore is interested in the news that William Burroughs is dead. And no one I know is any longer interested in the story of Burroughs being dead with me hanging around. But I am desperate now, and my only hope, in this sad world of vanishing interest in my anecdote, is that this will be the final and most decisive telling.

jure myself. The story is true—true-ish—but what had my enjoyment of the initial story added to its nature over time? A word to the wise: When you're pitching a big story over whiskey, it helps to throw in a few pieces of self-deprecation. The implication of my conversation with William Burroughs is that he wanted to tell me everything I could handle about Kerouac and his mother, but I, silly thicko limey visitor and pro-forma etiquette bum, stopped him for the sake of a better performance next day. The full effectiveness of my technique will be witnessed shortly.

William Burroughs was about to die, or, as a local sound-man attached to our crew preferred to put it, "the Beat god gone and died up on your ass." At the Harbourfront Festival in Toronto one time I'm sure I added Burroughs saying, "You're the boss" at the close of our telephone conversation. Well, I've checked the original journal. I've checked the television transcripts for references, but there's nothing. I can hear Burroughs saying Kerouac's mother was a witch in my head and I can imagine the telephone in my hand. But it didn't happen. It couldn't have happened or it would be in the journal and others would remember it. Over the years of telling the story it has become as real as air to me.

What happened was that Jim Grauerholz, who was Burroughs's manager, had suggested on the phone that William thought Kerouac's mother had made him drink. Then Wayne, a friend of Burroughs with an evil grin and a spanner in the back pocket of his dirty jeans, told me in the middle of a cornfield that Burroughs said how destructive Kerouac's relationship with his mother had been. My journal from the time notes Wayne saying, "Burroughs said it was pure hell." Wayne took us in a shed filled with smashed stuff and engine parts in order to get a beer (or, rather, we took our beers in there to get him) and I noticed a television screen that was smashed to smithereens. "Oh, that was William," he said. "He shot it last Thursday."

I add no spin to Wayne's character. Paradoxically, that is often what we mean when we say someone is like a character in a novel—we mean that no embellishment is required; the person exists so completely that no effort need be expended in describing or rendering them real. They exist. Well, Wayne was not a character in a novel but he had the force of one; his actuality came as a bit of a surprise and I knew that journalism could only struggle to catch him.

I have a strange tic of the imagination that would doubtless have led me straight to reform school if I'd ever confessed it to a child psychologist: Every time I've got a lethal weapon in my hand I spend a second or two picturing what it would be like to mow everybody down with it. Wayne offered me his gun at the edge of a cornfield. He set up a tin can and invited me to shoot it down. Now, I'm a pussy, so there was no way I was coming out of this one well, and I briefly contemplated killing everyone before I began firing at the can and missed it four times before clipping it with the fifth shot.

The motel was bad and hot during the night. When I told the story at a New York dinner party, I think I said the air-conditioning was broken all night. I don't think that's right. The air-conditioning was doing its best. I was tossing and turning with the shame, no doubt, of using five bullets to hit a can only ten feet away. The phone rang. It rang in that way that only Americans telephones do—as if someone somewhere is having a breakdown. It was the film's director. He said I should come to the foyer as something bad had happened. When I told the story to Patrice Hoffman, my French publisher, I'm sure I reminded him what film crews were like, and said I'd told the director to stop bullshitting and put down the phone. In fact, I got my shirt on and descended in the elevator immediately.

"Burroughs is dead," said the director. A person was there from the Burroughs world, not Jim Grauerholz, but usually for the purposes of narrative ease I say it was Jim. "He died at the hospital. He was taken in a day or two ago."

"So he was in there when we were with Wayne yesterday?" I think I asked.

"Yes," the director said.

Then something happened which I know to be true. The Burroughs person began saying he thought we should come to "William's house" and bring the cameras. Now, for my sins, and for everybody else's sins too, I'm a Catholic, and I do not think it's a good idea to poke cameras into the corners of the bereaved. My director, on the other hand, is a director: He knew there wasn't another BBC crew within a thousand miles, and he didn't want to pass up the chance to film Burroughs-in-death (as if anybody would have noticed the difference).

"No way," I said.

"William loved the BBC," said the man. "Come over to the house. He would've liked that."

I sometimes forget to tell this part when I'm telling the story. For a start I don't want the BBC to get too much credit, and secondly, when I'm telling the story I'm wary of things that—wait for it! wait for it!—seem made up. It just doesn't seem very credible that William Burroughs should love the BBC. But that's what the man said.

"I'll bring some flowers," I said, like Teresa of Avila, while Dave the director was semaphoring behind the Burroughs man for all he was worth. Every gesture Dave made was saying, "Don't do this to me."

"All of you come," said the man.

I think I said okay or Dave said okay. Anyhow, one of us said okay and we made arrangements to come to the house in Learnard Avenue at one o'clock.

Reality is insufficiently itself to command the complacency of the imagination. Wallace Stevens didn't say that, though he might have said it, give or take a few words. What we can be certain about is that he meant to say it. Reality is nothing without the imagination, like lungs without breath. The story about William Burroughs's death in Kansas is the story of something that actually happened; it is also the story of something that actually happened to me. That actuality has been tampered with and yet the story is no less real. It is more real. It has gone from being the-day-Burroughs-died to the-day-Burroughs-died-with-me-hanging-around to me-telling-the-story-about-the-day-Burroughs-died-with-me-hanging-around and now we are here, perhaps finally, at the place where all our favorite narratives are due to find their most ringing version: the-story-of-me-telling-the-story-about-the-day-Buroughs-died-with-me-hanging-around. Storytelling depends on the idea that there is a hierarchy of interest: Burroughs being dead was news (it was already playing over the radio as we drove to his house at 12:45), but it is a hierarchy that changes. No one anymore is interested in the news that William Burroughs is dead. And no one I know is any longer interested in the story of Burroughs being dead with me hanging around. But I am desperate now, and my only hope, in this sad world of vanishing interest in my anecdote, is that this will be the final and most decisive telling: the über-version, in which the story of William Burroughs's death at the age of eighty-three is nothing compared to the human business of me trying to tell the story of how I existed on the margins of this story and that I myself have become a margin on which stories fight for balance.

The house was definitely red. There was definitely a Merry Pranksters-style van painted with graffiti in the yard and a pond with fat goldfish swimming around. I asked the crew to hang back long enough to let me do my Catholic bit with the flowers. I laid them on the porch—there were three, four, already—and I pressed my face up against the flyscreen. There was a certain humming coming from inside the house; through the grayness I could see numberless cats flying in every direction. The humming was taking place at the other end of the room: chanting more than humming, moaning more than chanting. During an interview with a Stockholm newspaper I'm sure I once said the participants had their hands raised. They did not. Some of the people in the Buddhist circle have remained con-

stant from the days when I first told the story: Jim Grauerholz and John Giorno, the New York poet who was also, unfamously, the man asleep in Andy Warhol's film *Sleep*. Others have come and gone from the circle: The rock singer Patti Smith was there as far as my notes tell me, but I can't picture her anymore, and in all subsequent versions, including one I related a couple of months ago in London to an aging dowager under a long screaming pope by Francis Bacon, the figure most uncomfortably present in the circle was the agent Andrew Wylie.

Now, I've never met Andrew Wylie. I've always remembered him because he has the same name as the protagonist of *Sir Andrew Wylie of That Ilk*, a novel by the nineteenth-century Scottish genius (and Coleridge's favorite novelist) John Galt. A number of my friends are represented by Wylie, and one of them worked in his London office, but I have no relationship with him at all. I must have known that Wylie represented Burroughs, and known too that he had, in the days immediately after Burroughs's death, sold some final writing of Burroughs's to *The New Yorker* for a significant sum. That is just standard publishing gossip, but it must have entered my plan, because very soon after that I had Andrew Wylie sitting in the circle in Burroughs house while I stood at the flyscreen. Fiction had to somehow make up for a deficiency in the scene as it was being prepared for its distinguished career of retelling: Wylie was needed to bring the wonderful absurdity of the scene into its fullest dimensions: Somewhat gratuitously, I'd often have Wylie wearing a rather fat kipper tie during the ceremony that sent William Burroughs's soul out of the house. I've become so convinced of Andrew Wylie's presence in the scene that I can quite easily see his expression in the gloom; I can see him later standing on the porch in a white suit dabbing his brow, looking solemn. But Wylie seems to have been in New York that day. In fact, as any of my delighted listeners could have ascertained, Wylie could not have got to Lawrence,

Kansas, by one o'clock the day after his client died because you are unlikely to make the journey in that time. But I refuse to give up on Andrew Wylie: He is there in my perfect version of the story and he will remain there.

Then a doubt enters about my doubts. My journal from the time suddenly tells me this: "I saw a guy through the flyscreen. I thought it was Andrew Wylie, the literary agent in New York. They were moaning." So maybe Wylie was there after all. Maybe he came to see Burroughs before he died. Of course, as with all these things, I could, at any time during the last nine years, just have called Andrew Wylie to ask him, but that would have been, well, tactless, and not at all done in the spirit of my story. It is my story after all, and though I wouldn't want to deny anyone their own account of their own experience, I feel quite possessive about Andrew Wylie's whereabouts the day after William Burroughs died. He was in my story, humming or moaning or chanting.

The goldfish had a magic realist kind of life under the cool water of the pond and I wanted to join them. The crew stood around smoking cigarettes—in Spain I wanted to say they were joints, but I stopped short, recognizing how my thinking was drifting toward the teenage—and I spoke with one of the Burroughs people about the writing and the life that was over. He said one or two things about the hospitalization, then said that he had spoken to Gregory Corso that morning. Gregory wanted to come to Kansas for the funeral—Patti Smith was encouraging him—but he was worried about his methadone. "Oh, don't worry about that," someone chimed in, with a smile, "there's a ton of it here. Bill used to hoard it up in the garage just in case there was a nuclear war."

I'm afraid I'm not good enough to have made that up. Our summer had given itself to certain freedoms of mind, to an exhilaration that can come with freewheeling in and out of lives that were either going or gone, and we made hay. One seldom feels that same proximity of stories to the life of their telling, and sometimes I imagine that the whole summer was invented just for me to speak of it later, that there was no house and no TV crew and no Kansas either, just my own imagining of them. I promised myself a story, a factual one, when we set out on that journey in search of the storyteller's friends. But I had no notion of how it would give rise, as it has done, to my own unreliable narrator, a voice who lives inside me and who suspects facts and is happy to parse the life around him to suit his narrative instincts. He's my friend. I promised you a story and the promise never changes; it's the story that changes and improves like wine. That is why I am a novelist. Driving out of Kansas that day we left clouds of dust and laughter over the mysterious fields and a lone train made its way from Kansas to the world. We all disappear in the face of the facts. As Virginia Woolf was fond of saying, "Nothing is simply one thing." And so we drove out of Kansas without an inch of film.

Or did we fly? ∎

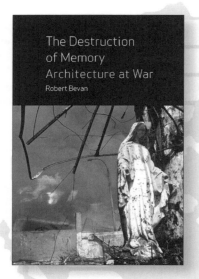

MILWAUKEE BUCKS

HOW A MIDWESTERN INDUSTRIAL FORTUNE CHANGED AMERICAN POLITICS

by Jim Arndorfer

IN 1958 AND 1959, in a dozen cities across the country, groups of businessmen huddled behind closed doors to hear a candy manufacturer's panicked warning. America was in peril from communism, he disclosed, but not in the way that many supposed. The red hordes were not at the gates—they were poisoning the United States from within. The civil rights movement, the unions, wayward educators: All these were working to deliver the USA to the reds. The candy man delivered his message with passion, and it took. His audience, chiefly small-time or middling manufacturers, had felt their blood pressure rise steadily in line with government's expansion since the New Deal. They didn't need much persuading to believe the speaker's labyrinthine conspiracy theories. Indeed, many heeded his call and enlisted in the organization he founded to spread the alarm. The speaker was Robert Welch and the organization was, of course, the John Birch Society.

One of the most smitten in Welch's audience was Harry Bradley, the top executive of the Allen-Bradley Company of Milwaukee, a maker of electronic controls. So inspired was he by one meeting that upon returning home he fired off a letter to Clarence Manion, the McCarthyite dean of the Notre Dame law school, whose desire to upend the liberal consensus of the day would drive him to agitate for a Goldwater presidential bid in 1960. "The reaction of all the participants was, I felt, strongly favorable," Harry wrote. "I know that for myself the two-day period constituted one of the most rewarding experiences of my life."

Bradley might not have been exaggerating his depth of feeling when he wrote these words. If anti-Communism and laissez-faire economics were the mid-century businessman's chief articles of faith, Harry was a zealot. He was the kind of man who lined his shelves with sober titles such as *Brain Washing in the High Schools, Roosevelt's Road to Russia,* and *McCarthyism: The Fight for America.* He greeted Nikita Khrushchev's 1959 visit to our shores with an ad in the *Wall Street Journal* reminding the nation that to the Russian boss, " 'Peace and Friendship' means the total enslavement of all nations, of all the peoples, of all things, under the God-denying Communist conspiracy of which he is the current czar." He didn't have much time for the New Deal and its legacies, either, and supported right-wing Republican candidates from Robert Taft to Barry Goldwater.

That was Harry: a square, a paranoid nut job, a dinosaur, a manufacturing chief. It's easy to regard him as a pathetic reminder of the way we were—until one pauses to reflect that Harry would have liked how American politics turned out in the coming decades. Pesky unions were beaten down. Government's biggest domestic job—pursued more assiduously than homeland defense—became cutting taxes. Deregulation and privatization came to be invoked to solve real and imagined crises. Yes, the shift in the country's business and political climate no doubt would have heartened Harry Bradley, who died in 1965. He would have been happier still to know that a key part in the counterrevolution was played by an organization that bears his and his brother's names. The biggest sugar

31

daddy of the American right since its founding in 1985, the Lynde and Harry Bradley Foundation has dispensed tens of millions of dollars to make Harry's once desperate dreams a reality.

I.

Harry entered business in 1903 when he joined Lynde at the electronics company his inventive brother had started with $1,000 in seed money from Stanton Allen. After years of scraping by, Allen-Bradley hit the jackpot selling motor control products during World War I. Business roared in the twenties. Like all manufacturers, Bradley was hammered during the early years of the Depression. But unlike thousands of manufacturers during those days, Allen-Bradley survived and was on the rebound by 1935. Economic turmoil wasn't the only specter haunting Harry. He grappled with another primal fear: that someone else, be it FDR's damnable New Deal bureaucrats or the insurgent unions organizing Milwaukee's factory workers, would tell him how to run his business. Unions in particular frightened him, and he worked hard to prevent them from getting a foothold. Besides engaging in the typical anti-union skullduggery, the company tried to woo its workers with generous fringe benefits—a reading room, Tuesday lunch hour concerts, and other early twentieth-century versions of Casual Friday. Harry

also made a heartfelt plea to his employees that a "direct personal relationship with the management . . . is more satisfactory than any relationship through a union."

Unfortunately for him, his workers—perhaps with past pay cuts in mind—disagreed. In 1937 Bradley's workers voted in not just any union, but one of the most militant: the United Electrical and Radio Workers of America. The Bradley brothers were even more shaken when workers struck—ultimately unsuccessfully—against the company's "open shop" policy. Poor Harry was booed by picketers; Lynde, according to the corporate history, looked down on the strikers from a window, saying, "What do they want?"

While thousands of factory owners across the country grappled with a distressingly restive workforce, the pain arguably was more acute in Milwaukee. Not only were unions strong in the "nation's toolbox"—Allis-Chalmers, the state's biggest employer, was a hotbed of militant unionism—but the city government itself had been hijacked in the early years of the century by honest-to-god Socialists. It was enough to force even a confirmed conservative to make a hard right turn, and plenty did. William Grede, owner of a major foundry of the same name, was a founding member of the Birch society (today the company's website baldly declares that unions have no place on the floor). Local industrialist William Brady would declare that capital "was man's best friend" and gripe that "unions do not create wealth. Their only purpose is to impose requirements and responsibilities on you that they have absolutely no obligation to fill."

Harry Bradley wasn't the kind who was content to merely grumble about big gummint over martinis at suburban parties. Along with Fred Loock, his right hand man and the real manager of the company, Harry sought nothing less than to wield Allen-Bradley's assets, human and financial, as weapons against Joe Stalin and his useful idiots in Washington. A 1952 memo Loock sent to employees summed up this apocalyptic worldview: "At the rate our government is spending—and we are paying—it won't be long before all money in excess of bare living will be taken away from us in Taxes, and except for the bureaucrats, you and I and everyone else will have become 'slaves of the state'—a title no one should be proud of." Indeed, he asserted, "we in this country are much farther along on the road to complete socialism than most of us are aware of."

The pair's fight to defend profits and the American Way came into high relief during the 1950s, as the Republican Party's conservative fringe chafed under Eisenhower. Allen-Bradley supported the *National Review*, which gave the far right a voice that was witty and urbane, as opposed to cracked and scary like the Birchers. (Harry was entranced with using the media to advance his politics. Bradley sponsored right-wing radio host Bob Siegrist, whose labor-bashing rants were broadcast across the Midwest. And, according to the Bradley corporate history, Harry once tried to buy the *Milwaukee Sentinel* and *Newsweek.*)

But Harry and Loock didn't just let their money talk. They also instilled the free-market ethos among management (a bit selectively, it would appear, as the company was nailed for price fixing in 1961) and rallied them to get involved in the political process. The company regularly dragged in political organizer Clif White (who would mastermind the effort to draft Barry Goldwater in 1964) to run seminars that whipped pencil pushers into rabid Republicans and, sometimes, politicians. Welch was called in to fire up the troops at sales meetings.

Harry was placed in a sanitarium in July 1960 after months of baffling and confrontational behavior. Fred Loock made sure that the company hewed to the boss's line in his absence. During Barry Goldwater's 1964 presidential bid—which presaged the Republican Party's shift to the hard right—Loock dumped copies of *A Choice Not an Echo* and *None Dare Call It Treason* onto his sales force with a note saying these potboilers "ought to be required reading." He also called for their distribution to "those many doubting Thomases

who still insist that 'it can't happen here.' " Loock cancelled advertising in *The Saturday Evening Post* after it ran an editorial knocking Goldwater.

Goldwater was annihilated in the 1964 presidential contest. Republicans got rolled in congressional contests as well. Indeed, between Goldwater's apparent willingness to drop the

A square, a paranoid, a Cold War dinosaur: Harry Bradley is an easy guy to mock. But he would have loved how American politics turned out a few decades after he died.

big one and exposés of the Birchers' paranoia, most Americans were terrified of the right. Worse yet, Lyndon B. Johnson was talking about building a Great Society and making the Fourteenth Amendment mean something.

It didn't seem like a world for Harry, who died at the age of eighty in July 1965. His mourners couldn't be blamed if they suspected his investment of time and money in the movement had been wasted.

II.

Such an appraisal would have been premature, however. Ronald Reagan's 1966 election as governor of California proved that there was life to the right after Goldwater's humiliation. And the opposition of Southern whites to the civil rights acts, along with the popular revulsion toward unwashed hippies and fear of crime, gave Republicans a base to build on. The emergence of the neoconservatives—ex-liberals or -leftists who'd seen the light—gave conservatism a patina of intellectual respectability. And while Richard Nixon in the Oval Office couldn't compare to the dream of a Goldwater White House, he wasn't Hubert Humphrey. And he sure as hell wasn't George McGovern.

But conservatives still lived in fear. Social movements from environmentalism to feminism threatened the nation's laws and businesses. Ralph Nader was flying the consumer flag and unions were getting uppity. Things were falling apart. The American Way needed a defender. And a rising chorus of voices, including leading neocon Irving Kristol, declared it was a job for business.

Corporate America, by and large, had stayed out of the country's political and cultural battles after the humiliation of the Great Depression. But this was no longer an option, according to Lewis F. Powell Jr., a Virginia corporate lawyer who served on the boards of eleven companies. In 1971, on the eve of his elevation to the Supreme Court, he did what any respectable executive would do when faced with a crisis: He wrote a memo—in this case a memo that predicted how the right would seek to set the terms of national debate.

"No thoughtful person can question that the American economic system is under

broad attack," Powell asserted in his legendary note to the U.S. Chamber of Commerce. But it wasn't the Yippies who were the real threat: It was the "hostility of respectable liberal and social reformers. It is the sum total of their views and influence which could indeed fatally weaken or destroy the system." So far business leaders had "shown little stomach for hard-nose contest with their critics, and little skill in effective intellectual and philosophical debate." But that had to change. The Chamber, Powell proposed, should enlist a staff of scholars and speakers ("preferably attractive, articulate, and well-informed") to defend the market and provide a counterweight to slanted professors; monitor textbooks and the media for bias; churn out books upholding the system to counter works "advocating everything from revolution to erotic free love"; and hire lawyers to press business interests in the courts.

The U.S. Chamber didn't act on Powell's suggestions, but others took his warning to heart. The memo "stirred up" right-wing beer baron Joseph Coors, who shelled out $250,000 to launch a Washington-based think tank called the Analysis and Research Association—known now as the Heritage Foundation. Heritage soon began sucking in millions in donations from Pittsburgh billionaire Richard Mellon Scaife and other spiritual descendants of Harry. Within fifteen years, a phalanx of other think tanks, foundations, and legal action groups were checkbooked into existence by business interests. Older standard bearers, such as the American Enterprise Institute, got in step with the new direction. The scent of money quickly attracted swarms of bright young conservative things, not to mention established scholars, eager to cross swords with the libs.

Soon America was treated to the spectacle of tax-subsidized propaganda mills that attacked the various gains and protections that working people had won over the past century. Legal foundations assailed environmental regulations. Think tanks derided unions, denounced social programs, praised hostile takeovers, and called for rolling back taxes for the rich. The Cato Institute started calling for the privatization of Social Security. At the Heritage Foundation, larval wonks churned out position papers on hundreds of topics assembly-line style. Despite their lofty titles, these think tanks were not models of intellectual rigor or honest inquiry. "We're not here to be some kind of PhD committee giving equal time," a Heritage vice president declared in 1986 to *The Atlantic Monthly*. "Our role is to provide conservative policy makers with arguments to bolster our side."

The objectives of all this think tankery would have been familiar to right-wingers of Harry's vintage. But the unseemly redbaiting of the past had been ditched. Now rhetoric focused on enhancing opportunity and freedom for all. Still, for years Heritage and its ilk were beyond the pale of serious discourse. It took the election of Ronald Reagan in 1980 to put this demimonde in the driver's seat of policy. The Reagan Administration adopted a wide range of think-tank proposals for remaking government. Just as importantly, think tankers were hired to fill policy positions in the Reagan and Bush Administrations. Think tanks also provided sinecures for old government hands. By the time Newt Gingrich unveiled the *Contract With America* in 1994, the winger ideosphere had become a political ascendancy.

One of the young stars of this movement was Michael Joyce. Born in 1942 to an Irish-Catholic family in Cleveland, Joyce grew disaffected with his clan's Democratic politics and in 1972 voted for Nixon. He made another switch soon after, leaving the teaching profession to take the top job at the Goldseker Foundation in Baltimore. But it was in 1978 that he truly began his ascent in the neocon universe, moving to New York to head up the Institute for Educational Affairs, an organization Kristol and former Treasury Secretary William Simon founded to provide cushy thinking jobs for right-wing college students and other young conservatives. (In 1988, the institute started Dinesh D'Souza on his lifelong addiction to foundation cash by giving him a $30,000 taste for a book project.) The next year Joyce hit the big time when Simon tapped him to head the John M. Olin Foundation, an offshoot of a family chemical and munitions business that was one of the premier funders of the right. As further proof that the working-class kid from Cleveland was made, he was appointed to the Reagan transition team in 1980.

A compact and pugnacious super-Catholic, Joyce had a taste for controversy and unshakeable confidence in himself and the cause. "To the extent that the neoconservative movement has any strength," he said in 1985, "it's not in numbers, but in sparking debate." Spark it he did when Olin bankrolled sociologist Charles Murray to write *Losing Ground*. Published in 1984 and backed by a PR blitz, the book argued that welfare didn't ameliorate or end poverty, it merely encouraged laziness and urban pathology. Loaded with charts, the book was a hit with the Reagan White House and its message was embraced by a wide swath of the media—notwithstanding the fact its argument relied on dubious statistics, flawed methodology, and bogus claims. Debunked but not discredited, Murray's arguments were to help shape the welfare reform debate of the early nineties.

> **Lewis Powell, later a Supreme Court justice, wrote that American businessmen should fund right-wing scholars to counter a left that advocated "everything from revolution to erotic free love."**

III.

The conservative movement already had plenty of reliable millionaire donors when the shareholders of Allen-Bradley sold out to the defense conglomerate Rockwell International in 1985. For Milwaukee, whose industrial core had been decimated by the recession of the early 1980s, the sale was yet another blow to civic pride. But it turned out to be a windfall for the right wing.

One of the biggest beneficiaries of the sale was the Allen-Bradley Foundation. Created in 1942 after Lynde died, the foundation gave primarily to hospitals, colleges, and youth organizations. (Being part of the Bradley world, it also disbursed cash to wingnut groups like the Manion Forum, the Freedoms Foundation, and Morality in Media). At the time it was just another podunk foundation with about $14 million in assets. But as the sole beneficiary of the Margaret Loock Trust (the wife of Fred), the sale inflated the foundation's assets to more than $290 million.

The foundation proceeded to sever its ties to the manufacturer. becoming the Lynde and Harry Bradley Foundation. But the biggest shift was in its mission. Under the guidance of chairman I. Andrew "Tiny" Rader and director William Brady (who in 1956 had started his own foundation, which grandly took the motto "Ideas have consequences"), the Bradley Foundation would shift its scope of operations from provincial Milwaukee to national policy. As Rader explained: "The principles Harry believed in gave us the strongest economy, the highest living standard, and the greatest individual freedom in the world. We felt that it was our task to do everything we could do to preserve those principles."

Acting on Harry's principles meant funding winger schemes. And to fulfill this mission, the Milwaukeeans brought in the dynamic Michael Joyce. Joyce made full use of his expanded arsenal, blasting away at creeping socialism wherever it could be found or imagined. Joyce and Bradley established ties with conservative heavyweights from Bill Bennett to William Kristol and swiftly gained a reputation as a central force of the conservative movement. Upon Joyce's retirement in 2001, a *Wall Street Journal* editorial spoke for many when it gushed, "There's scarcely a part of America's culture that Bradley hasn't touched—and left the better for it." Joyce died in 2006.

This praise wasn't hyperbole. The foundation has poured tens of millions of dollars onto a wide range of conservative causes, money that simply hadn't been available before. From 1985 to 2003 it funneled $13.2 million into the Heritage Foundation and $15.9 million into the American Enterprise Institute, the two chief conservative think tanks, according to figures from Media Transparency. It also fronted $2.2 million for the Federalist Society, the right-wing legal frat that numbers forty thousand lawyers and business people (plus five thousand law students), and whose membership rolls include such illustrious government officers as Ted Olson, Samuel Alito, Antonin Scalia and many, many more. The group held a conference in 2001 called "Rolling Back the New Deal." Millions more have been handed out

to a rogues gallery of cranks, ranging from Paul Weyrich, who still bemoans the Communist infiltration of the *New York Times*, to David Horowitz, the self-promoting terror of college newspapers.

Joyce played no small role in the rightwing sniping of the early nineties, when a constellation of talk radio chin-waggers and think tank scribblers upped the ante of political attacks on liberalism. It supported the publisher of the *American Spectator*, fount of some of the nuttiest attacks on Bill Clinton. In 1992 it slipped nearly $12,000 to Heritage so it could provide sustenance for David Brock as he expanded an article bashing Anita Hill and defending Clarence Thomas into his notorious book *The Real Anita Hill*.

Bradley also dished out $1 million to Joyce's old comrade Charles Murray as he and Richard Herrnstein ground out *The Bell Curve: Intelligence and Class Structure in American Life*. Published in that revolutionary year of 1994, the book purported to demonstrate through regression analysis that poor folks—particularly African-Americans—were at the bottom of the heap because they were dumb. Launched with a massive publicity blitz, the book received some favorable, if heavily caveated, reviews from conservatives such as Charles Krauthammer and William

Bennett. *The New Republic* actually treated it as a matter worthy of serious discussion.

Bradley also subsidized the intellectual spadework that would one day come to fruition in the Bush administration's invasion of Iraq. As detailed in an April 2003 article in the *Milwaukee Journal-Sentinel*, Bradley was a significant funder for William Kristol's New Citizenship Project Inc., which created the Project for a New American Century. This group, which included Dick Cheney, Donald Rumsfeld, and I. Lewis Libby, was an early advocate of imposing regime change on Iraq, a position it articulated well before 9/11.

Bradley has also thrown some swag to the hawkish Committee for Peace and Security in the Gulf. The American Enterprise Institute, one of Bradley's favorite wards, has provided much of the theorizing behind White House policy. And Bradley has long been a supporter of Harvard University's John M. Olin Center for Strategic Studies, which was led until 2000 by Samuel P. Huntington, whose *The Clash of Civilizations* has nourished a Manichean view of conflict between the Islamic world and the West. On the home front, it has funded Daniel Pipes' Middle East Forum, which has blasted college professors and students for opposing the war in Iraq.

But Bradley's obsessions have always been rolling back and discrediting the public sphere and encouraging the privatization of public services. It has chosen its most prominent fights on its home turf of Wisconsin and Milwaukee. Bradley has looked upon the city and state as free-market "reformers" eyed post-Soviet Russia: as patients on which to test their most radical treatments. Thus did the home of La Follette and the Milwaukee Socialists become a laboratory for right wing economics.

The fight to privatize welfare—in which Wisconsin was way out in front of the rest of the country, a distinction for which most observers credit Bradley—demonstrates how the foundation's bucks influenced the debate. Bradley was a major funder of the Wisconsin Policy Research Institute, which routinely bashed the welfare system. It also poured $4.2 million into the Hudson Institute, the Indianapolis think tank that smoked up the so-called Wisconsin Works program. Right-wing talk show host Charlie Sykes, who has been on the Bradley payroll, flacked the Bradley-funded program. (Wisconsin Works, sold as a way "to build a bridge to meaningful work for the poor," and pushed through by a Republican governor, has produced results that fall far short of its advertising. While the executives of private agencies administering the program have seen their paychecks skyrocket, "clients" have not been placed in good jobs. A study published in May 2006 found that few earned enough through work and benefits to rise above the poverty line.)

Meanwhile, Bradley has moved on to another neocon cause célèbre in Milwaukee, shelling out more than $15 million to support Milwaukee's school voucher program, paying legal bills to defend it in court challenges and establishing scholarship programs. While originally sold as a means of improving the lot of minority inner-city kids—and Bradley did tap into genuine concerns about the state of schools—Joyce clearly viewed the voucher program as a means of broadly undermining public education. "It is my opinion this will be a hot story," Joyce wrote to Kristol, then Vice President Quayle's chief of staff, as recounted in Nina J. Easton's *Gang of Five: Leaders at the Center of the Conservative Ascendancy.* "It pits poor, unorganized urban minority parents against the established power of school bureaucracies, unions, old line civil rights organizations, and the advocates of special interests." (Joyce himself didn't mind middle class or rich kids participating in voucher programs and said: "I don't think public funds should be used to support schools at all. Public funds should be used to support the parents' provision of education for their children.") The heat continues, more than ten years after the program took root. Milwaukee public schools haven't collapsed as some doomsayers predicted. But vouchers *have* drained sorely needed re-

sources from a cash-strapped school system. And there's an ongoing fight to expand access to the program beyond the poor kids it was ostensibly designed to save.

Bradley wielded its cash to reorder domestic social policy, but it also aimed to change the very vocabulary of public policy discussions. Chroniclers of the conservative movement during the eighties such as Gregg Easterbrook have noted how right-wing think tanks and intellectuals redefined the national dialogue about the role of the private and public sectors and the relation of capital to society. Their efforts went a long way toward creating a consensus view that the market was the best solution to society's ills. Local organizations, the Bradleyans believe, are the ones best equipped to tackle local problems, and faraway governments can only muck things up. Indeed, Joyce and his henchmen loved to blame the Progressives and Herbert Croly for many of today's social breakdowns, arguing that turn-of-the-century calls for a national community wiped away a utopian world in which community-based organizations wisely dealt with problems from the neighborhood drunk to juvenile delinquents. It's a worldview that calls to mind Marx's illustrations of a communitarian prehistory, and it's just about as realistic. Churches and private local institutions just know the needy better than any bureaucrat ever could, and they are motivated by a quality no bureaucrat could ever have: compassion.

Bradley thus played a crucial role in introducing one of the most risible currents of American conservatism. Marvin Olasky, a born-again professor of journalism at the

University of Texas, was a Bradley Fellow at Heritage when he wrote *The Tragedy of American Compassion*, which, upon its publication in 1992, introduced the notion of "compassionate conservatism." Olasky's thesis is that charity worked great when it was run by churches that "suffered with" the poor and made them work for their gruel; charity went to hell when religious groups and governments began to regard welfare as a right, not a privilege. For compassionate preachers like Olasky, deindustrialization, racism, poor education, and urban rot are not meaningful topics when discussing poverty; nor are the ways in which social factors have shaped charity and relief programs. What matters to Olasky are anecdotes illustrating how private charity is good and government (some aspects excepted) is bad. Tough-love church charities that force the indigent to chop wood for their keep have the right idea. Olasky's book caught the eye first of Newt Gingrich and then of political operative Karl Rove, who made it part of George W. Bush's rhetorical repertoire.

Dismantling the safety net in the name of compassion: It's a subtler argument than likening the New Deal to the Bolsheviks' NEP—and a more effective one than anything thought up by the Goldwaterites. Who's against compassion? Indeed, the Bradley Foundation court history takes pains to draw distinctions between the thinking of Harry Bradley and the brain trust now ensconced at the foundation bearing his name:

> The conservatives of Harry Bradley's era tended to be tract writers and podium thumpers, long on convictions but short on intellectual curiosity. Joyce is quite the opposite. He is careful, first of all, to distinguish between ideologies and ideas. An ideology, any ideology, begins and ends as a faith, an object of simple moral commitment. Ideas, on the other hand, begin as potential truths; they are the morally neutral medium of intellectual discovery. . . . It is the world of ideas that Joyce and his associates navigate. In contrast to the religionists of the 1950s, they operate with the intellectual precision of theologians.

One wonders what, say, Thomas Aquinas would have thought about the Bradley Foundation propping up a hack like Murray. Yet in their professions of distance from the raving right-wingers of the past, one senses that the foundation of today protests a little too much. To be sure, ideas have consequences—but only if they are ultimately translated into action. And if the cool thinkers of today are accomplishing the ends desired by Harry and other hothouse wingers of the past, does it matter what intellectual constructs they use to achieve these ends?

In the past thirty years, the right has seized the mantle of reform and enlisted it in the cause of capital. Joyce and a host of think tank janissaries have stood the impulse of the Progressive Era on its head. Wielding corporate dollars and taking advantage of U.S. tax law, they have spent three decades rolling back the reforms working people won—and men like Harry Bradley opposed—in the century before. Harry is gone, but his money goes marching on. ∎

BUY AND HOLD 'EM

by Kim Phillips-Fein

For "joe_hill"

In the mornings and afternoons, Salvador is a stay-at-home dad, something of a rarity in his small Midwestern city. (The names and online names of players have been changed.) He plays with his one-year-old son, feeds him lunch, and settles him in for a nap, while his wife punches the clock as a sales rep for a pharmaceutical company. But in the evening, after she comes home from work, Salvador goes to the computer. There, far away from the shimmer of Vegas, in a quiet corner of his house, he settles in for the long night of poker that, he says, recently won his family a large new home.

Salvador—he picked the name, he explains, because he's a Dali fan who likes to think he can turn a surreal play now and again—makes his money in ten-player online poker tournaments known as sit-and-goes. He has a 21-inch LCD monitor on which he can play four or more games at once; sometimes, he will play as many as six hands of poker simultaneously. His library consists of nearly 250 books on hold 'em, gambling, blackjack, and Las Vegas. He owns a software database that records all the hands he plays, so that he can study them later, and he regularly contributes to an online chat room about all matters related to implied odds, fold equity, semi-bluffs, and inflection points. Poker isn't Salvador's only game. He likes counting cards at casino blackjack, too. "Any gambling game that I can gain an edge at mentally, I will play," he says. But poker is the game he's worked hardest to master, and it is far and away his most profitable. In the past year and a half, he's averaged $150 per hour.

Before he became a poker professional, Salvador sold tires. On the side he worked as a DJ, playing weddings and parties and sometimes working ninety-hour weeks. He grew up an army brat, living everywhere from Virginia to Panama. Although he's enrolled in a stray course or two over the years, he doesn't have a college degree. Online gambling, though, has changed all that. Today, he says, "my wife will mention to doctors that her husband plays poker for a living. Now, I have doctors and lawyers asking me questions about what I do."

For someone like Salvador, poker is no desperate gamble. Rather, it is a claim on middle-class respectability, an entrée into a world of meritocracy.

In the American imagination there is no other game like poker. Its roots, like those of baseball, go far back into our past. Historians think it entered the United States, via New Orleans, as a variant of an eighteenth-century French game called *poque* blended with a Persian game known as *as nas* ("the beloved ace"). The rules of the game were codified in the 1870s, when Robert C. Schenck, a congressman, Civil War general, and ambassador to Britain, wrote a treatise on poker to teach Queen Victoria how to play the game. But no one can pinpoint a single inventor, making it seem as though the swirl of money and dreams in the early years of the Republic generated the game all by itself. Part of what has always made the game so alluring is the way it reflects our cultural ambivalence about wealth. Poker highlights the contingency of money, the way that it comes and goes with luck. It shows the emptiness of riches, denied to some, lavished on others with the capriciousness of fate, making a mockery of hard work and talent. The game's fickleness and its lack of regulation make cheating a perpetual lure, as much a part of poker mythology as the royal flush.

The popularity of gambling games seems to move in cycles as manic as the ebb and flow of the stock market. Last century's poker was faro, a strange game played by dealing cards out of a box. Faro's main attraction was the exceptionally favorable odds it offered the player. Yet as a result of those favorable odds, the temptation for the box holder (known as the banker) to cheat at faro was all but irresistible, as this was the only way to make a profit. As a result, the game came to resemble the economy of the Gilded Age, in which a market open to all came to be dominated by a few, whose economic power derived from chicanery and sheer force.

The current poker boom is about thirty years old, and in peculiar ways it mirrors our modern economy, just as faro did that of a century ago. Today's poker hysteria began in the early seventies, when Ted Binion, an enterprising Las Vegas casino owner, began to organize what he called the World Series of Poker. A parade of colorful characters gave flavor to the rediscovered game, figures like the three hundred–pound evangelical Christian Doyle Brunson, author of *Super System: A Course in Power Poker, or, How I Made Over $1,000,000 Playing Poker*, a bible-thick 1978 book of gambling strategies; and David Sklansky, a Columbia math professor's kid who likes to boast of having taken up poker after dropping out of a promising actuarial career.

But it was only in the nineties, as the punk rockers went to work for Arthur Andersen and wealth became part of the sleek, hip yoga of Clintonism, that the poker craze came into its own. Triumph in the marketplace began to be seen as an expression of one's inner genius, the opposite of selling out, and poker took its inevitable place in the fantasy. Perhaps the best example is the mid-nineties Matt Damon movie *Rounders*, which defined

poker for the dot-com era the way *The Cincinnati Kid* did for the sixties. Damon plays a lackadaisical law student, seemingly on his way to becoming the Man, who also has a strange ability to read other people's cards, most notably those of his professors at their home games. The movie carefully distinguishes Damon's poker brilliance from the hustling of an ex-con friend, from the low-stakes grinding of a friend who ekes out a living in underground card rooms, and from the nihilistic, brutal gaming of a local Russian Mafioso who owns an illegal poker hall. Damon's skills at the poker table blow the rest of these characters away, and the movie ends with him dropping out of law school and heading for Vegas to make an honest living.

We learn that the world of poker is noble and fair, unleashing pure intellectual talent in a way that the respectability, academic hierarchy, and dreary routine of law school never can.

Today, rumors of *Rounders 2* circulate on the Internet. In one parody of the imagined sequel, Damon winds up in Vegas and, staking the wrong buddy, falls $15,000 into debt. He hops in his car to go find the high-stakes games. But just when it seems he might be about to hit the Strip, he instead picks up a hot sub from the local Quizno's and drives home. There he opens his laptop and proceeds to play eight tables of poker at once. After some marathon sessions, he makes the money back. It's the same movie, but minus the glamour, which somehow seems appropriate for a post-stock-market crash sequel. The eager novices dreaming of Dow 36,000 get their trading accounts cleaned out; the condo flippers find themselves suddenly, inextricably "upside down." Getting by—surviving—is all that's left, and it's a grind.

The transformation of poker has a lot to do with its movement out of Vegas and Atlantic City and onto the computer screen. In the images presented by ESPN and peddled by magazines like *Cardplayer*, the game is no longer a matter of luck and fickle fate. Instead, it is a new arena of pure competition, a space for libertarian fantasies of skill and merit. The *New York Times* runs feature articles on poker as a rags-to-riches story, where even the humblest ex-theater major can win a seat at the World Series. *The New Yorker* publishes salivating profiles of young poker celebrities dripping with cash. More people are playing poker for greater stakes—and the game is making far, far more money for the house than ever before. For as poker has shed its shady connotations and become integrated into the mythos of the market, it has also become a game in which the house—the owners of the casino—can become fantastically wealthy, far richer than even the most successful poker player.

In the old days, casino owners never really liked poker. Unlike all the other familiar gambling games—craps, blackjack, slots, roulette—poker does not offer the house a lucrative advantage. The players vie against each other rather than against the casino, which has no way of getting a piece of the action except to skim off a portion of every pot. This is why poker tables in most casinos were hard to find. They were tucked away in the back of the house, and to get to them you had to walk past the mirrored slot machines and the wild-patterned carpets, the soft green felt of the blackjack tables, and the steady whir of the roulette wheel. The house hoped you'd be distracted by the shine and flash before you made it to the cramped, badly lit card rooms, crowded with people who looked like they hadn't moved for days. Today, although casinos sometimes advertise poker, building off the online buzz, they still hope that the kids who come in to play will be lured into pursuits more profitable to the house.

In the great gamble that was the late nineties, however, the owners of online poker websites managed to flop a full house. The Internet has made poker safe for investors. There's no need to pay for labor or land when the dealer is a randomizing algorithm, and as a result, the game is nearly pure profit for the house. The biggest online site, bearing the dignified name Party Poker, earned revenues of nearly $400 million in 2004.

Online poker, with all its contradictions—luck and labor, glamour and boredom—is a fitting game for an era of political defeat and widening social inequality.

When it went public in June 2005, its market capitalization skyrocketed to more than $8 billion, making it overnight one of the largest companies to trade on the London Exchange. The identities of Party Poker's founders were released in the buildup to the IPO—the company turns out to have been started by a former online porn star and her South Asian computer programmer buddy, Anurag Dikshit, whose last name delights poker chat rooms everywhere.

The other big-time poker firms are privately held and release little information. No one seems to know who owns them, and most are headquartered offshore in places like Costa Rica. Online poker's legal status remains murky in the United States. Hosting tens of thousands of players every night, the online "gaming" industry has made enemies ranging from New York Attorney General Eliot Spitzer to Focus on the Family's James Dobson. As this goes to press, two bills are circulating in the House of Representatives that would effectively make playing online poker in the United States illegal. (Party Poker, not surprisingly, is vigorously lobbying against the legislation; the company has helped to form a "Poker Players Alliance" that distributes T-shirts emblazoned with the slogan: "Poker: An American Tradition. Keep

It Legal.") But for the time being, the tidal wave of money has undoubtedly mitigated the legal concerns for most investors. According to *Barron's*, the online poker industry was expected to gross $2 billion in 2005—compared to $5 billion in gambling revenues for all the extravagant palaces on the Las Vegas Strip. Even top-flight investment banking companies like Goldman Sachs and Morgan Stanley are starting to buy shares of online poker companies.

At the other end of the table are the ever-increasing ranks of people like Salvador, who have taken up poker as a second career. In the aftermath of the tech-market collapse, poker has surfaced as a different way to make money online. As bestsellers about day-trading give way to paperbacks about MIT students cleaning up in Atlantic City, it is clear that the poker craze is the half-life of the stock market boom, sustaining many of the same fantasies about capitalism. But for people like Salvador, poker seems less like the ESPN fantasy of instant riches; it is instead a steady second job, a moral theater where tenacious work and book-smarts can pay off. The game thus represents to its devotees both a perfect market, where talent cuts across all obstacles to make deserving people rich, and, at the same time, an escape from the vicious realities of the market as we know it today.

Previous installments of poker mania celebrated the game as a deeply personal contest, a sort of psychological combat between flamboyant figures in which individual peculiarities counted for everything. Gambling narratives were a form of amateur philosophy. In one of his poker memoirs, for example, Doyle Brunson writes of driving from Lubbock to Amarillo in search of a profitable game. "If you've never had occasion to travel a two-lane county highway through the Texas panhandle, you don't know what it means to be lonely," he sighs, describing life on the gaming frontier during the "dark ages of poker" in 1961. The unflappable Brunson wanders through a world of sketchy characters, men in love with cash, desperate to flaunt it and furious when it gets lost. He exploits their emotional ups and downs and takes their money. There is, of course, honor among gamblers: Brunson says he would never hire a lawyer, and that when you shake hands with a gambler, you know you'll get your money by sunset if you win the bet. "Poker is a game of people," he pronounces. "If you remember that, you can bounce your opponents around like tumbleweeds in Texas. If you forget, Lord have mercy on your bankroll."

As Brunson knew quite well, poker has always been a game of calculating probability

as much as reading character. But as it is played today, poker has less and less to do with people—in online poker, there are no faces to read, just icons on a screen. Instead of observing a furrow of a brow, a tap of a foot, you catch your opponent's bluff by close attention to his or her betting pattern. Indeed, periodic rumors circulate about the presence of "bots" in the online games—robots trained to raise the bet whenever they get two aces. Today's poker players are bookish types, avid students of the game. Poker is traditionally about risk, chance, and gamble, but today's online players seem to love the game precisely because it is so predictable.[*] Sure, your heart quickens when you look down and see two aces in the hole, but at the same time, you know it happens to everyone once out of every 220 hands. Over the long run, seasoned players love to intone, everyone gets the same cards.

In keeping with this mechanical view of the game, the poker websites do without excessive adornment. The graphics are rudimentary, little better than the video games of the early eighties. Typically, they depict ring games of six to ten players, often including stock poker figures like the guy in the cowboy hat and the blonde wearing a low-cut red dress. Frequently the "dealer" is a brown-skinned figure in a tuxedo. On some sites you can request that a very pixellated "drink" be brought to your seat at the table. Professional players barely notice the graphics, however; they're too busy playing six or eight games at a time, using two or even three monitors, making the long run arrive that much faster. Instead of relying on memory alone, they also use elaborate database programs that import information about their opponents' style of play, so that they can see right away how likely it is that a given player will fold to a check-raise or hang on until the river card.

For online grinders, poker is in some ways like a desk job, monotonous and filled with tedium. The game is relentless, involving, as it must, endless hours of agonizing over the right play at the right moment. Players worry about the same health hazards that afflict the office worker: eye strain, carpal tunnel syndrome. On poker discussion sites, players

> In the images presented by ESPN and peddled by magazines, the game is no longer a matter of luck and fickle fate. Instead, it is a new arena of pure competition, a space for libertarian fantasies of skill and merit.

complain of a growing sense of hold 'em fatigue: "I make more than twice as much at poker than I would at any job I could find," writes one typical player. But "I don't enjoy online poker anymore." And yet at the same time, the repetition of the game alternates with wild swings that can resemble low-grade emotional torture. How many part-time jobs are there where you can go to work, do everything right, and yet lose thousands of dollars in a night?

To mitigate the swings, some players turn to what they affectionately call "bonus whoring," the cyberspace equivalent of the Vegas type who lives for "comp" meals in the casino cafeteria. For these resourceful cheapskates, poker is little more than a high-tech coupon-clipping system. It works like this: As new poker websites try to muscle their way to prominence, and more established ones seek to hold on to their player base, they often offer cash bonuses to regular players, or else what is gracefully called "rakeback," in which some proportion of the "rake" that the web-

---

[*]The version of the game favored by today's online poker players, Texas hold 'em, has a surface simplicity that distinguishes it from such favorites of yore as stud and draw. Each player receives two cards face down, and then five more are dealt face up, the point of the game being to make the best five-card hand. This suits it well for online gambling, since one can easily play multiple hands at once without getting confused.

site takes from each pot is refunded to the favored player. Players who have learned how to "bonus whore" can make money (albeit not Bellagio-style riches) without doing much more than breaking even at the game. Of course, the websites have now begun cracking down on bonus abuse, requiring ever more ingenious mastery of bureaucratic procedure by the players.

How different the workaday reality turns out to be from the breathless hype doled out by ESPN. Even for the players who succeed most dramatically at the game, it can come to feel as much a burden as a joy. Consider James, twenty-eight, who lives in the Williamsburg section of Brooklyn, land of hipsters and cheap beer. James went to Brown, and in the late nineties he worked as a journalist and tech analyst for a small firm that covered start-up companies. But then the bubble burst and the start-ups stopped. James turned to what he knew—the Internet. He now earns $400,000 a year playing online poker—usually $30/$60 limit hold 'em. "When I got laid off and started playing, it was enough to help me buy extra drinks," he says. "Then it was enough to take all my friends to dinner." Instead of huddling in a smoky back room of a casino waiting to play a few hands, James now has access to anonymous opponents at any hour of the day or night. Yet despite living the poker dream, James says he finds the game at once boring and addictive. He can't pick up a book, he says, without mentally calculating how much money he could make online in the time it will take him to finish it. "Every hour is commodified, in a way," he muses. It's a prosaic view, far from the lonely roads of the Texas panhandle.

Just as the poker economy divides into the grinders and the high-stakes players, there are also sharply differing ideological visions of the game. On the TV programs and in the official interpretations offered by poker writers and magazine editors, poker demonstrates—as all things must—the superiority of capitalism, the glories of the market. The darker aspects of the game—the fact that for every winning player, there must be many who lose—are interpreted as a sign of the market's justice. And there are numerous players who share these ideas, adopting wholeheartedly the view of the game as a ruthless competition for riches and glory. But there are others for whom poker comes to resemble a countercultural alternative to the corporate world, a space—strange as it may seem—of professional autonomy, a fleeting realm of freedom.

In addition to the chatter about the correct way to play Q10 offsuit and the talk about which database analysis program is best, poker chat rooms occasionally offer reflection on the ethics and meaning of the game. Players have discussed forming a poker players union, which would be able to bargain with the website owners for better terms of play (this idea came up after a few sites announced that they would no longer offer the coveted rakeback). The idea was discarded after someone pointed out the inherent obstacles to organizing a strike: If all the pros stopped playing, the remaining players would be "fish" (i.e., weak players), causing any pro worth his or her killer instinct to want immediately back into the game. The structure of competition undermines any hope of improving everyone's position through collective action. Meanwhile the über-predator—the house—is simply beyond challenge. (Not everyone has given up,

though—some players now talk about starting a rake-free site, sort of like the producers' co-operatives of the late nineteenth century.)

The players you encounter in poker chat rooms are likely to be overall winners at the game, and from time to time they talk about the morality of playing online poker for a living—and especially about the strangers whose money they take. Much of the time, players respond defensively to any suggestion that they are doing something wrong. They are, they say, simply playing a game and winning, like anyone in the market. They fantasize about the people they beat, the ones they'd like to think they are righteously taking down: high school kids stealing their parents' credit cards, college students playing for a lark, rich brokers looking for a little after-hours action. In spring 2005, one player asked, "Are we not, as habitually winning poker players, bigger leeches on society than people that abuse the unemployment/welfare program?" After all, he continued, "We are taking money straight from the pockets of other people." The responses flew fast. Winning players were like entrepreneurs, insisted one enterprising showman: "Poker players provide the same service that any entertainer provides. You pay them money, and they entertain you." Someone who had chosen the online name of "Freudian" described poker as the inevitable separating of the unfit from their cash. His opponents, he observed, "would only have bought crack and beer with the money anyway." Another player said that he'd recently asked his priest about the morality of winning his living at poker. The priest, he reported, had determined that as long as the other players had "the same opportunities for improvement," there was nothing wrong with beating them. And one particularly savage player offered this distillation of libertarian sadism:

> I am a vampire, I rob others of their life energy and life force in order to exalt my own. The same reason they can't afford shoes is the same reason mine shine. . . . One's living quality will always be the result of the critical decisions they make, and poker is brutally honest.

But not all players share these views. For others, poker comes to seem something more like a "modernist avant-garde," a world of outsiders who float alongside "real" society, independent of its petty mores. Poker has its literature, its jargon of wheels and flops and crabs and cowboys. Its greatest attraction may be less the promise of riches and fame than

In a world of inherited privilege, poker can seem like a true meritocracy, democratic in a way the real marketplace can never be.

that of subsistence won without a boss leaning over your shoulder. Poker, writes one player, is "one of the purer forms of socialism, in that it acts as a wealth transfer from rich stupid people to poor smart ones." It is a kind of craft or trade, writes another: "Winning poker players have a skill that they have worked for." Asked what poker contributes to society, one player counters by saying that many people who work "aren't really contributing anything either. But since they have a 'job,' that is O.K." Extrapolating from this point, another player observes, "managers, by definition, don't make anything of value, but there are way too many of them." In a world of inherited privilege, poker comes to seem like a true meritocracy, democratic in a way that the real marketplace can never be; in a world of humiliating or dead-end or soul-killing jobs, as strange as it may seem, online poker becomes the repository of dreams of independence.

Money floats free of labor in online poker. It is a place of pure circulation, skimmed off of the fat of the land. But there is also a world of labor that lurks outside of the poker game and which shadows it like a nightmare. Here gambling seems like a stable second job, with players bouncing from table to table in the hope of getting an extra hundred bucks to make the rent. This is the reality in which everyone's lives are supposed to reflect their rational choices, and in which, at the same time, finding a decent, humane job sometimes seems about as realistic as flopping a royal flush. By these standards, poker is not a rebel's gamble, a game of capitalism's flip side, but instead—as improbable as it seems—a form of aspiration in which hard work and pluck might actually, someday, pay off. There is a certain desperation behind this idea of poker as the ultimate test of the marketplace—the hint of disappointment and failure beneath the bravado, the ghosts of other dreams that have not worked out. Online poker, with all its contradictions—luck and labor, glamour and boredom—is a fitting game for an era of political defeat and widening social inequality. For even as it thumbs its nose at class and respectability, with every hand, predictable as rain, the players re-enact the fables of perfect competition that the market has always told about itself. ∎

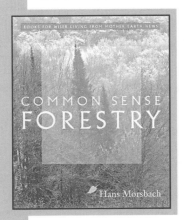

FOUR MINUTES AND 33 PAIRS OF SWEATPANTS

by Martin Riker

You're both musicians, so I'll put it to you in musical terms. Certain people have volume problems, simply. They have what you might call an awkward sense of dynamics. They're loud when the rest of us are soft, and when the rest of us are loud, they fall silent. And this man, Byron Brandt, was just such a person, a social misfit in the most literal sense. His part in the story of my life is hardly more than laughable, yet tied by fate to the end of my time with Peter Smith, which wasn't laughable at all. I don't mean to say that Peter's leaving was tragic, exactly. It just happened, as I remember. What's Eliot's line? Not with a bang but a whimper.

Oh, I do realize he's a small-time celebrity now, and a sort of idol of yours, but understand that when I first met Peter Smith he was just another struggling artist in his twenties, same as me. Of course, there are always plenty of struggling artists in their twenties. If Peter and I were different, which we were, it's because we were both intensely committed to what we were calling "real life." We believed that the most interesting art was that which engaged matter-of-factly with the most quotidian human events—work, play, eating, and sleeping, rather than just sex and death—and this idea, which probably sounds old-hat to you but seemed rather new-hat at the time, this idea was what brought us together. It set us apart from others and made us feel that we were working "beyond the rat race," as Peter said. It put us on a different track, a fact that gave us a great sense of freedom coupled with a perhaps greater sense of futility and fear.

That Peter was a closed-off person, very private, was never a real problem. But we also disagreed about art, the one thing that mattered. I was interested in concepts, you see, while Peter was primarily concerned with material things, making, building. He didn't have a lot of respect for "ideas," although he kept this particular opinion to himself, or tried to, out of his feelings for me.

I haven't forgotten Byron, by the way. We'll get to him in a minute.

I'd been living with Peter for three years when I woke one day to the realization that I was twenty-seven, working four jobs just to pay our bills, and had nothing to show for myself artistically. You can imagine what a terrible day that was. It put me in a state of panic and self-doubt. I became obsessed with my own lack of productivity, my fear of failure, and all this anxiety only made it harder for me to get work done. I mean artistic work. If I didn't talk with Peter about this, which I didn't, that's because I held him partly responsible—the circumstances of our lives together had distracted me from my own goals. Oddly enough, in reading his recent autobiography I've learned that Peter had a similar feeling at the time. Can you imagine finding out something like that from an autobiography? I was the one working four jobs, though, so I don't see what he had to complain about.

At any rate, it was during this difficult period that I first spoke to—here we are—Byron Brandt, the man people called "the Astor Place crier." He was always standing under the Astor Place cube ranting about one thing or another, anti-corporate this and ideological that, and so naturally I thought he was an art student. And he dressed eccentrically, a yellow bathing suit and sandals . . . and nothing else! Well, it was a gimmick. He claimed that his body was as naked as his truths, a slogan that became more desperately uninteresting each time he repeated it. He obviously intended to shock, to provoke. In reality, he turned out to be *shy*, but of that particular shyness that manifests itself as extreme, even obnoxious, extroversion.

At that time I was working at Carl Fischer Music in the afternoons, and so would pass him on my way to work. I'd always assumed he was a lunatic, which he was—Socrates in a swimsuit, with his endless catalog of rants, accusations, affronts, all the so-called "passionate" rhetoric that passes for the real. A lot of it having to do with music, though, which is why sometimes, walking past, I would listen, and why one day I decided to respond.

It was, I remember, a particularly miserable day, miserably hot, but also my mood was worse than usual. For some reason my personal frustrations had chosen that day to collide with my general sense of the futility of all artistic enterprise, so that I was predisposed, climbing up out of the subway station, to view anything I might run into as a mockery of my life. And there he was, his shrill voice and ridiculous outfit, claiming

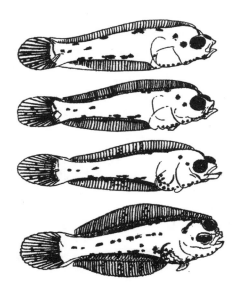

that music was the basis of all human experience. Since I was early for work, I walked over to him. Music, he was saying, was the "alpha discourse," it was the "crème de la discourse" because it "said nothing," and "*Nothing*," he announced, "*is the superior thing to say.*" It was a high-spirited if not very nuanced argument, and an ironic claim from a man who apparently never stopped talking.

I imagine he was used to being ignored, one strange voice in a city of strange voices. I imagine having someone actually stop and pay attention must have been a rare experience for him, although my presence there did not slow him down. If anything he spoke faster, like a nervous schoolboy at a spelling bee. Having established that music "says nothing," he proceeded to liken everything in life to it—food and shelter, love and laundry, science and sports—as if drawing analogies to music somehow made more sense than likening all the same things to, for example, the weather. Gertrude Stein tells us "comparisons are odious," and as usual she is absolutely right. Comparisons *are* odious—they're so easy and plentiful! A point our politicians understand very well. Byron, of course, was no politician. His ego was too erratic, for one, too up and down and up and down. I don't mean to make him sound like a complete buffoon. . . . He wasn't. . . . Well, he was, but the art world is filled with such people. He, at least, had the courage of his idiotic convictions.

There I was, though, growing more irritated with each of his shabby comparisons, imagining each a personal attack on my own self-worth. As he finished he turned to me provocatively, an arched-eyebrow look, as if I should wither from the heat of his fiery confidence. It was a very male gesture for a very male sort of foolishness, and so of course he was surprised when, instead of submitting to his absurdities, I decided to point them out: He wanted life to be music so that it wouldn't have to be life. It wasn't that he'd faced chaos and now wished upon it music's quasi-mathematical coherence. It wasn't that he'd struggled with the set of values that had been handed to him and found these values ultimately insufficient to human feeling, and so sought a system more beautiful and correct. It wasn't that he cared about life *at all*, I told him, he just liked talking, and he believed he'd found something to say that would be hard to argue with. We all assert ourselves in one way or another, and this was the form he'd chosen. Which, I said, was fine as far as it went, but he should understand that, for anyone who cared about music and ideas, who worked very hard and tried to take her life very seriously, it was a frustrating, embarrassing display.

He seemed to shrink while I was talking, and when I was done he stayed silent. He wore an awful look of stupefaction, as if his erratic ego, his ego which pumped like a human heart—expanding to blood-filled hugeness only to collapse, then expand, then collapse—as if this ego had suddenly stopped mid-beat. If "nothing" was the superior thing to say, then Byron didn't say it very well—*his* nothing was as obvious and vapid as his speech! Of course, I hadn't meant to hurt his feelings, and when I saw how sensitive he was, I felt bad for what I'd said. I'd taken out my problems on this poor ridiculous person. This total stranger. I'd never even stopped to talk to him before.

The following afternoon I avoided Astor Place, approaching the Carl Fischer building from the south. I had no desire to see Byron again, but, alas, *he* found *me*, came into the store, up to my counter—somehow he'd found out that I worked there—and erupted with all of the refutations and rebuttals he'd apparently been rehearsing since the previous day. He didn't get through very many before the manager and a security guard threw him out—too loud, and of course there were rules about dress—but by then any guilt I might have felt had turned to worry and anger at my own stupidity. I realized I'd bred a beast, and that this would not be the end of him.

Sure enough, he showed up the following day, dressed this time in long pants, a long-sleeved shirt, dress shoes, and a jacket. He found me working in the stacks. Right away he began listing his objections and clarifications, none of which I currently remember, although I stood there listening—I listened and listened and agreed with everything he said. I wasn't about to argue. I told him he was right, whatever he was saying, I'd simply been confused, lost in my own problems, but certainly the world and everything in it was related to music and not to anything else. He wouldn't let it go, though. He scoffed and insisted, underscored and reiterated, because the truth—which I only fully realized later—the truth was that Byron was less concerned with whether music was in fact the basis of all human experience than with whether or not I was impressed that he thought so.

After that, he would come into the store a few times a week dressed in his nice outfit, or would find me outside during my break time, always with new claims and fresh rebuttals, until finally I realized what was going on: He was *courting me*. In his twisted ridiculous mind these pseudo-intellectual harangues were supposed to attract me, like colorful plumage. This was of course something I had no interest in at all. I should have just turned him away, but I didn't have the heart to, and he was either too shy or not self-aware enough to just *come out with it*, so instead we played this game. I started mentioning "my fiancé, Peter" as often as possible, thinking Byron's crush would naturally pass. Peter and I were never actually engaged, but this was meant to strike a note of finality. I told him about Peter's favorite foods, his little quirks, his plans to take me to Spain for our honeymoon—most of it lies, although I did dream of going to Spain. Or I'd talk about picnics Peter and I had taken in the park, or in the country, also made up. I was so *dreamy* about it, I almost convinced myself. At any rate, it had its effect. Every time I mentioned Peter, Byron would grow irritated, scoff, and storm off muttering.

If I was interested in Byron, which I suppose I was, this was only because he was so completely different from Peter. Where Peter

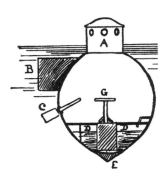

was shielded and private, Byron was out there for all to see. You perhaps felt that you saw *too much* of him, but there was nonetheless this availability, this *loudness*, which was only partly off-putting, and only because of the second-rate quality of his mind. In truth, between my exhausting work schedule and Peter's relative seclusion, my conversations with Byron were the only opportunities I had to discuss my various ideas about music and life and work, and so, mostly by default, this time became important to me. I didn't love him, though. I never loved him. That he loved me was just another anxiety to deal with on top of all the others.

Now, given all the forces at work in my life at that time, you would think that I didn't get any composing done at all, yes? And yet it was during this period that I wrote what would become my first work of any consequence, the performance piece "Four Minutes and 33 Pairs of Sweatpants." The idea came because Peter was unemployed at the time and would sit around the apartment all day in his sweatpants, working on his instruments. Since I was holding down four jobs and had hardly any time for my own work, the sweatpants became a source of irritation for me, a symbol of my frustration. I would come home between jobs and find him still in his sweatpants. I'd say, "Please tell me you're not *still* in your sweatpants," and Peter would say, "I'm not *still* in my sweatpants, I *changed into* my sweatpants." What he meant was that he'd changed from one pair of sweatpants into another—whether this con-

stitutes "changing" or is simply a form of staying the same is a question I leave for the philosophers. Suffice it to say that Peter had more pairs of sweatpants than anyone I've ever met, as if he'd been collecting them all his life, which I think he possibly had.

The concept behind "Four Minutes" was simple enough: a composition in the form of a competition, the prize for which was the opportunity to make music. I've always been drawn to the idea of musical compositions *about* making music, because making music is something that I care about, and I enjoy making art out of things that I care about, but in retrospect I recognize the limitations of this particular work. It was solvable, for one, and was eventually solved, and so now is forgotten. I freely admit that it was a showy piece. I admitted it at the time, but saw no reason why an artwork could not afford to be a little showy as long as it produced something interesting.

The performance would take place in a large room, an auditorium or theater. There would be a stage filled with instruments of all types and sizes, and many items that were not at that time even considered instruments, including some of Peter's own creations—a collection capable of making every sound imaginable, or at least the most beautiful ones. The performer would stand on the right side of the stage where a pile of sweatpants had been stacked, thirty-three in total. Thirty-three being the number of pairs I'd found in Peter's sweatpants drawer. Once given the signal—my shouting "Go!"—the performer had four minutes in which to play anything he wished on any of the instruments assembled, provided he first accomplish the seemingly simple but in reality nearly impossible task of putting on every single pair of sweatpants. Thirty-three pairs in less than four minutes was to be rewarded with total creative freedom within the remaining time. I didn't bother to stipulate that the performer would also take the sweatpants *off*, since it never occurred to me that anyone could wear thirty-three pairs concurrently. Or rather, it occurred to me several times that no one possibly could.

Needless to say, the sweatpants allusion was not wasted on Peter. I imagine that he resented it, although all he said about the piece was that it wasn't a "composition," it was just an "idea," and that I was "buying into the whole competition business," which meant that the piece "wasn't really art." It was the only time he'd directly criticized my work, and was the beginning of the end for us. I should have stood my aesthetic ground but was too angry to think, and so ended up arguing on his own pathetically practical terms. I said I didn't have *time* to work on a "composition" because one of us had to make "money," and this *fact* was what my "idea" was about, which made it a rather appropriate sort of "art," didn't he think?

Apparently, he did not. A textbook prima donna, Peter thought everything was about him, whereas in reality only a very small part of that composition—a simple detail, a stage prop—had to do with him at all. And even the sweatpants were not chosen to mock Peter, but because the task of climbing into thirty-three pairs of them was so obviously ridiculous. If I was mocking anything, which I was, it was my own life, the grueling boredom of my daily tasks and the absurdity of my own anger, this anger that had chosen to manifest itself in resentment toward, of all things, Peter's sweatpants. It was not about our relationship so much as relationships in general, these types of banal frustrations that

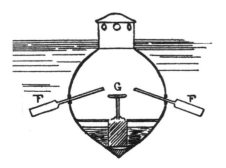

persist between people in love. I suppose our own relationship might have fared better had I told Peter some of this. But he never said a word about the sweatpants, so I never got a chance to explain.

There followed a moment of indecision, a day or two when my life might have gone a different way. "Four Minutes" was something new, an exciting possibility, but it was making things worse with Peter, who for so long had been the most important person in my life. . . . Well, I suppose you can second-guess anything, particularly in hindsight. If I'm going to be honest, there's no way I could have stopped, even if I'd wanted to. Which I didn't. "Four Minutes" was mine, after all. I'd conceived it, for what it was worth.

Peter, meanwhile, had become almost irritatingly cooperative. Deciding to play the martyr, he put aside his own feelings and helped me stage the first performance. We had no budget at all. We used a community auditorium that a friend had access to, and Peter took charge of assembling the instruments, some of which we had, some we made, most of which we borrowed. His generosity ended at his sweatpants, which he categorically refused to lend. In fact, he grew angry when I asked. This was a bit of a setback, although I suppose I could see his point. I took care of coordinating the performance—originally there was going to be just one, at most two—which meant hanging fliers all around town, an enumerated Martin Luther-type manifesto I'd composed, numbered points about the challenges to artistic production in the modern age along with an official announcement of the event, a call for participants, and a kind of tear-off and mail-in sign-up sheet. Within a week forty-five people had mailed in, mostly men. We got an extension on the space, scheduled five performances per night, and decided to charge admission.

Attendance was good from the start. On the first night, some art and music critics showed, those reporter types who write for the papers, and soon there was an unbelievable "buzz" around town. The piece moved into a larger space, but we were still turning people away. We bought a bell to signal "Go!" and some friends signed on to screen applicants. It was surprising how fast it all happened—it was absurd, truly—and it soured Peter on the project once and for all. He was right in what he said: People liked it for the wrong reasons. He didn't mean this as a criticism of me. It was a joke to them, a good time. He stopped coming after the first week. He took back his instruments, and then, suddenly, he was gone, from the piece and from my life—just like that. His departure went almost entirely unmarked, as I remember. No fanfare, hardly even any feelings. We'd been together for three years. I suppose it was over well before that.

At any rate, the piece quickly grew into a bona fide cultural phenomenon, everyone was having a good time, and I started to make money from it. Not *much* money, but enough to give me courage to quit my various jobs and concentrate on other projects. Since I was never around Astor Place anymore, I stopped seeing Byron, and, frankly, didn't give him much thought. At the same time—and this seems strange to me even in retrospect—I also started gaining a reputation as a promising conceptual artist, even though, as far as I could tell, no one took the piece seriously or considered it anything more than a glorified parlor game. I won't say this realization didn't bother me, just as I won't claim that Peter wasn't finally right about a lot of what he said. But I was caught up in success. And with Peter suddenly out of the picture—he'd taken his sweat-

pants and moved to New Jersey—it seemed the only thing that mattered to me or anyone in my life was the fact that no one could get in and out of thirty-three separate pairs of sweatpants in under four minutes' time.

And this was the state of affairs when one night Byron showed up, dressed in his old yellow bathing suit. The piece had been running for just over a month by then, although it seemed much longer. He walked straight up to me, his face straining to look righteous, his finger pointed to look accusing. He claimed I'd "abandoned him" for my art—which was basically true—that I'd "stolen his ideas"—which was absurd—but that he'd come, now, to set things straight. He'd been "working the problem," had "solved our furious enigma," and would "demonstrate the ease of it." I found his bravura maddening, but it turned out he'd mailed in an application and been accepted through the normal channels, so there was nothing to do but let him make a fool of himself.

He was third in the line-up, which was actually one of the better spots to fill—the audience was warmed up by then, and not yet tired. Since Byron was already a sort of local joke-celebrity, there was a considerable amount of cheering when he got onstage, although nothing as loud as Byron himself, who went on about a wide range of asinine topics interspersed with claims that he'd "prepared something very special" for when he'd "surmounted" all the sweatpants. Meanwhile, I stood in the back of the hall, pretending it wasn't me he was looking at.

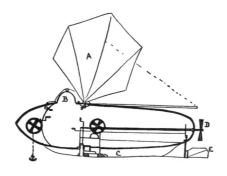

Of course I knew what Byron was up to, that he was planning, one way or another, to express his love for me. I saw this from the moment he walked in the door. But while I was not anxious to find out what sort of "music" Byron's love might conjure up, neither was I particularly worried that I'd have to.

Then the bell rang, the clock started, the crowd settled down. Byron began normally enough, though what struck me right away was that, while he put the sweatpants on in the usual way, he didn't take any pairs *off,* he just kept layering. We'd seen this strategy before, of course. Early on, a few competitors had tried to squeeze into four or five pairs before pulling off the bunch, but this method proved cumbersome and ended up taking more time rather than less. With Byron, though, we watched as he passed pairs three and four and continued to pair seven, eight, and on. As each pair stretched tighter, the chances of getting out of them grew slimmer, and so when he reached the eleventh pair, and there was obviously no going beyond it, I assumed the performance was done. Being dim-witted—I told myself—Byron had imagined he would keep going, that he would somehow magically fit into thirty-three pairs of sweatpants simultaneously, but instead he'd just managed to look like a fool.

Well, I underestimated him. Byron, it turned out, had a unique talent—I mean a talent unique not just to him but to that particular situation as well—he had the otherwise useless ability to wriggle out of eleven pairs of sweatpants in no time at all. If that doesn't sound very impressive to you, I suggest you try it sometime. I, who've seen it happen, still haven't the slightest idea how it was done. I can tell you that he was lying down, that the movements involved were disturbing to watch and even more to listen to, that the audience was silent and utterly amazed, and that I personally experienced every possible emotion, one after the other in just a few minute's time—but beyond this, all I know is that he managed it. Eleven pairs of sweatpants!

He went on, of course, and reached the

thirty-third pair, the final pair of the last eleven, with twenty-five seconds to spare. He didn't bother to take the last eleven off, but simply moved himself as he was to center stage. The sight was met with silent, bewildered anticipation from everyone there. For my own part, I was excited to see what he'd do, which instrument he'd choose, what sort of music he would make with it. It had occurred to me, during the extraordinary emotional rollercoaster of the preceding minutes, that this was a chance for my piece to reclaim itself, to demonstrate to the world that there was a *purpose* to this tiresome exercise, a goal greater than the intentionally absurd task of fitting into a pile of sweatpants. It was only then, on the verge of Byron's success, that I discovered how much such validation meant to me. I'd been through a great deal, after all, not just the sacrifice of the previous months but the struggle of previous years, all the work that goes into the creation of a single exceptional moment. So, I was excited. I hoped he might choose something beautiful, like an oboe—one of the more difficult instruments to play, but at that instant he seemed capable of anything. I said to myself, "If he picks up the oboe, I could love him." But do you know what he picked up?

Nothing. He didn't say or play a damn thing, he just stood there, staring out into the crowd, at *me* in the back of the room, with an expression as blank and stupid as when I'd first questioned him under the Astor Place cube. And while I'll never know exactly which "nothing" he thought he was performing that day, I know which one I was witnessing. He looked frightened, terrified even, as if, having come all this way, the weight of his "mysterious" message had landed on his head and struck him dumb. For me, it was more revolting to watch than all the bizarre contortions his strange body could ever produce. I hated him. I wanted to throw things at him. He was wasting an artistic opportunity. He was *mocking* it. He might as well have spit in my face.

When his time was up, I slipped out, walked home, and went to sleep. I have no idea how the evening ended for everyone else.

Peter, it seems, left the next year. He joined the Army—I've just been reading about it. We weren't talking by that point, and I didn't hear of him again for almost twenty years, when his touring ensemble started appearing in art magazines. They play here in the city sometimes. I've attended once or twice, incognito. It's interesting to read his book, to find out what happened to him, even if it is his own version. Our life together was several lifetimes ago, you understand, so there are no hard feelings. In fact, there are no feelings at all—how could there be? There couldn't.

As for Byron, after that night he could no longer be found around Astor Place or anywhere else. I never saw him again. I can't say I've missed him, or that I've given him much thought. He was an interesting man conceptually, the idea of him was interesting, but as a thing in the world he left a lot to be desired.

And while, looking back, I can't say "Four Minutes" was my finest work by any measure, it was, I think, the best work I could have done at the time. It was silly, on one level, but on another it was a rather serious and intimate composition about work and art and the personal struggles I faced throughout my twenties. It was composed out of those struggles, as a way to make a space for myself in all the dull commotion.

Now, of course, it's completely forgotten. And just as well. After that night there was no point to it anymore, it held no interest for either the audience or me, and the world moved on to other things. I know many artists, writers, and composers who hate their early pieces because their popularity overshadows later, better works. I know others who are true one-hit wonders and happily ride their singular wave into oblivion. I know artists who crave fame and others who despise it. I know some, riddled with pettiness and insecurities, who assume that everyone else is just as petty and self-absorbed, and I find these people only slightly less absurd than those who believe they are emotionally unique. I don't know where I fall among such categories. At different times, I've fallen differently. I know that at one time "Four Minutes" was an important part of my life, that later I grew to resent it, that for a long time now it's been as if someone else wrote it, and at moments I've been sorry they bothered. But there it is, either you make something or you don't. ∎

THE CARLYLE GROUP

Is
so
powerful
so rich

and so private
they
say
nobody

not even
their opponents
knows
where

they play
tennis

—Geoffrey Young

FREE (MARKET) VERSE

by Steve Evans

WHEN JAMES MERRILL DIED ten years ago, the *New York Times Magazine* used the occasion to publish an obituary—not of the elegant poet himself but of the entire "poetry establishment." Without Merrill's inherited millions trickling down to fellow poets, the magazine predicted, the clubby uptown world of old-style patronage would soon unravel. Donor readings at J.P. Morgan's former home, easy access to the pages of *The New Yorker*, cushy tenured chairs, guaranteed publication by FSG and Knopf, and a monopoly on prestige- and cash-conferring prizes—all of it would disappear in short order. Meanwhile, barbarians were at the gate—L=A=N=G=U=A=G=E poets, Hip-Hop poets, Neo-Formalists, Surrealists, Nuyorican slam poets—and it wasn't another exquisitely crafted, emotionally muted poem that they were clamoring for.

One can forgive the *Times Magazine* for failing to notice that a sort of reactionary party was forming as well, one with its own axe to grind for the poetry "establishment." Fronted by a trio of Midwestern white guys with business backgrounds, this nascent movement envisioned a revolution in American poetry, a renaissance of good old-fashioned verse about authentic American life for the amusement and improvement of regular folks. Metrical, memorizable, mom-and-pop approved, the poetry these men dreamt of would make easy money out of easy meaning, enabling poets to earn their keep on the free market rather than depend upon millionaires' sons or MFA programs to subsidize them. According to them, once poetry was fully deregulated, once its creative and entrepreneurial forces were freed

from the fetters of state patronage and academia alike, good and true voices would reclaim the audience that obscurantist snobs had forfeited sometime circa 1910.

The tiny band of businessmen bards gained little ground in the waning Clinton years. But with the ascension of George W. Bush, things started breaking their way. Led by men like Dana Gioia, John Barr, and Ted Kooser, the movement has forced its distinctive blend of economic elitism and cultural populism onto the poetic map. Making the entire, unlikely effort possible was an act of dumbfounding eccentricity: a curiously timed gift to Chicago's *Poetry* magazine from a pharmaceutical heir who, before she slipped into four decades of crippling depression, had submitted a pseudonymous item or two to the review, which politely rejected them.

When Ruth Lilly dropped a $100 million gift on *Poetry* in the late fall of 2002, what astonished people most was the sheer size of the sum. Though she bestowed even more money on an organization called Americans for the Arts, the idea that a quaintly penurious outfit like *Poetry* should come into such unexpected riches appealed to the journalistic imagination. The charming, Dickensian narrative involved shabby, sunless quarters in a library basement inhabited by a chain-smoking, lunch-skipping editor who had for decades heroically sacrificed all to the culling—from ninety thousand submissions a year—of the few poems good enough to earn the magazine's $2 a line and be brought before the eyes of its subscribers. Now, through her mysterious beneficence, Lilly had lifted *Poetry* from this place of squalor and cultural obsolescence. From a grandparent warehoused in a seedy retirement home, the magazine had been transformed into the newest and richest kid on the block, its financial capital now far exceeding the dwindling symbolic capital it had been husbanding since the days of first-wave modernism.

Poetry may be "news that stays news," as Ezra Pound, an early contributor to *Poetry,* once asserted, but it has a hell of a time cracking into an actual news cycle. That the story of the Lilly bequest had such tremendous newsworthiness was no doubt due to the way it fused two terms held to be incompatible since at least the Romantic period: poetry and money. The novelty of the conjunction, and the eccentric manner in which it came about—the frail and reclusive Lilly, most of whose life has been spent under psychiatric care, had her lawyer handle everything, reminding some of the old television series *The Millionaire*—made for good, or rather *feel*-good, copy.

The good feelings back in November 2002 might have been harder to sustain if any of the journalists covering the bequest had bothered to connect it to another bit of news concerning Eli Lilly & Company. The corporation, a longstanding supporter of Republican politicians and an indirect backer, through the Lilly Endowment, of the usual conservative causes, came into a bit of luck of its own. The Republicans had just prevailed in the midterm elections, lending legitimacy to George W. Bush's presidency and ratifying his post-9/11 makeover into a wartime commander-in-chief. Shortly after the results were in, four paragraphs were appended—no one could say by whom—to the 475-page Homeland Security bill then under consideration in Congress, paragraphs exempting the Lilly Company from lawsuits (*The American Prospect* foresaw a "torrent" of them) related to the manufacture of thimerosal, a preservative added to vaccines that was then suspected of being a possible cause of autism.

How bulletproofing a Big Pharma concern made the homeland safer, again, no one

could say. But the action could not have come at a better time for Lilly. Having lost its bid to extend the patent on Prozac, the company had been stumbling badly that year. Faced with competition from generic alternatives for the first time since its introduction to the U.S. market, Prozac sales had fallen off by 70 percent. With no blockbusters anywhere near introduction, and with the threat of litigation over thimerosal growing more serious, Lilly's share price had taken an ominous downturn.

In fact, between January 2002, when Ruth Lilly revised her estate plan and funded the bequest to *Poetry*, and December 2002, weeks after the bequest was publicly announced, the 3.8 million shares of Lilly stock that formed the basis for the gift had declined in value by 36 percent. Worse still, National City Bank of Indiana, which handled the trusts that funded the bequest, botched the sell-off of the stock so badly that Americans for the Arts and *Poetry* sued for negligence and breach of fiduciary duty.

So at least two important facts never made it into the heartwarming story of Ruth Lilly's handout to *Poetry* magazine. The bequest was timed to coincide with a scandalous political payoff that had been snuck into the Homeland Security bill and hurriedly signed into law by Bush. Second, by the time it was made public, the bequest itself was already the object of bitter litigation by its beneficiaries.

Poets for Bush

Several other developments around that time rhymed with the *Poetry* bequest. In September 2002, the poet Ed Hirsch was picked to preside over the John Simon Guggenheim Foundation, effectively putting him in charge

of about $7 million in grant monies per year. The following month, the neo-formalist businessman poet Dana Gioia, who takes credit for revitalizing the sales of Jell-O and Kool-Aid during a stint in the marketing department at General Foods, was named to head the National Endowment for the Arts, which distributes about $100 million in grants to organizations, state agencies, and a dwindling number of individual artists each year.

Each man interpreted his ascension as a sign that reason was slowly being restored to a poetry world that had addled its collective brain in academic workshops, bogged itself down with postmodern claptrap, and attended for far too long to degrees and CV-lines in default of its duty to be "accessible." Hirsch, an aesthetically conservative poetry insider who left the University of Houston to take up the Guggenheim post, lamented his genre's self-inflicted wounds. "Poetry hasn't been well served by poets who fled to the margins," he told the *New York Times*, exhibiting a handy knack for construing effects (poetry's marginal status in the capitalist infotainment order) as causes (it's poets who *fled* to the margins).

Gioia's fame stems more from an attack he launched on the inbred subculture of academic poetry in 1991 than from any serious interest in his own verse, and he has continued to trumpet accessibility ever since. "I still write more for my old fellow workers [at General Foods], who will never read my poems, than for the literati," he has said. He is also—as the magazine *Workforce Management* put it—a welcome "corrective contrast to the tired stereotype of an eccentric or anti-establishment artist."

According to a squib in *Variety*, "Some Washington insiders speculated that first lady Laura Bush, an avid supporter of the arts and letters, had a hand in tapping Gioia" for the NEA chairmanship. If that was the case, Gioia kept mum about it in public—less out of modesty, one suspects, than because his fellow poets were in full throat opposing the Bush administration's plans for war in Iraq.

Indeed, the Senate confirmed Gioia on January 29, 2003, just two weeks before a gala dinner at which the first lady had hoped to demonstrate her admiration for the rhyming arts in the company of culture-war hawk Lynne Cheney and a group of poets that included Sam Hamill. When the militant pacifist (and ex-Marine) Hamill not only de-

> No Midas could transform this meager stuff into good poetry. This is not because the poems are populist in intention. It is because they are almost entirely devoid of verbal wit, cognitive surprise, or strong passions.

clined to attend but decided to counter-program a "day of poetry against the war" for February 12, the East Wing event—which may have been intended as a coming-out party for Gioia—was summarily scrapped.

As Hamill gathered thousands of antiwar poems for presentation to Congress (some thirteen thousand had come in by March 1), Gioia spent the first months at the NEA dodging questions about the poetry community's lack of support for his patron's imperial adventure. Even the politically quiescent Billy Collins, then serving as poet laureate, publicly expressed distaste for the gathering storm of "shock and awe." But Gioia stubbornly maintained his silence. When pressed, he responded with a defensive generalization, arguing that if poetry is considered "only as conceptual, ideological speech, it diminishes its role as art." It was amusing, in a way, to see the bright-eyed champion of clarity, accessibility, and familiar forms being driven into the arms of aesthetic indeterminacy by a spontaneous and overwhelming outbreak of plain-speaking dissent.

Deregulating Poetry

The tiny but powerfully placed band of businessmen poets continued to grow when, in February 2004, the organization established to administer *Poetry* magazine's Prozac millions named an investment banker, John Barr, to be its new president. (Joseph Parisi, the longtime editor of the magazine, had been set to lead the foundation, but he returned from a vacation in the summer of 2003 apparently having thought better of it.) Like Gioia—described by Barr as a "kindred spirit" with whom he bonded "because we could both read balance sheets and had this love for poetry"—Barr leans heavily on his

dual background when speaking to reporters, whose fawning stories on him always seem to run under half-clever headlines like "A Passion for Poetry, and Profits" or "Invested in Poetic Currency." Consider the following, which appeared in the respectable pages of the *Christian Science Monitor*:

> When John Barr, president of the Poetry Foundation, enters a room, the image that comes to mind is "live wire." Make that "power line," since Barr, formerly an investment banker known for structuring complex utility deals, seems to have great energy beneath a cool exterior. His quick smile and striking white hair add to the impression that he doesn't just occupy a room, he commands it.

At least all those electricity metaphors underscore the fact, usually overlooked by reporters at cultural desks, that Barr made his fortune in the business sector whose leading light was Enron. Indeed, Barr was one of the founders of Enron's chief competitor, Dyn-

egy, which followed the leader into complex but questionable utility deals and then into a near-catastrophic tailspin, with its share price falling 95 percent in 2002. Barr does not himself appear to have participated in any Enron-style looting of consumers, investors, and municipalities. But his ability to surf the waves of energy deregulation, first at Morgan Stanley, then in his "boutique" mergers-and-acquisitions firm Barr Devlin, does testify to an apparent love for the game of privatizing public resources, minimizing citizen oversight of decisions that affect them, and exporting the laissez-faire model abroad. "I think poets should be imperialists," Barr once told an interviewer. "I think they should be importers; I think they should be exploiters of external experience, without apology. I don't see that kind of thinking very often in the poetry world."*

Are the skills that allow one to extract profits from a newly deregulated field also useful in the world of poetry? Does the argot of mergers and acquisitions have any purchase in the thickly populated and relatively decentralized territory of twenty-first century verse? It takes but a small feat of metaphorical imagination to get to yes. And it is here that the MBA poets, like Gioia and Barr, have shown some flashes of brilliance largely absent from their poems. For when they cast a cold eye over the poetry industry, over the toilers who staff the increasingly routinized creative-writing programs, churning out two or three thousand MFAs in poetry per annum, they see a market in need of shaking up.

In "Can Poetry Matter?" the 1991 blueprint for deregulating poetry that he took with him to the NEA, Gioia castigates the artificially propped-up institutional market for poems: "Like subsidized farming that grows food no one wants, a poetry industry has been created to serve the interests of the pro-

---

* To judge from his campaign donations, Barr's politics are typical of the Republican-dominated oil and gas industry, where more than three-quarters of contributions flow to the GOP. Alternately giving as his occupation "investor," "retired," "self-employed," and "poet," Barr opened his checkbook almost exclusively to Republican candidates between 1994 and 2004 (the one exception being a Republican who turned independent to run against another Republican).

ducers and not the consumers." And just as David Horowitz enlists civil rights language in his struggle to end college campus discrimination against God-fearing white kids, Gioia swipes a page from the opposition by converting anti-academicism—usually the weapon of bohemians, avant-gardists, and other writers from the social margins—to his own purposes. He even cites Karl Marx as his authority for the following nugget of class-conscious analysis: "In poetry's case . . . socioeconomic changes have led to a divided literary culture: the superabundance of poetry within a small class and the impoverishment outside it. One might even say that outside the classroom—where society demands that the two groups interact—poets and the common reader are no longer on speaking terms."

Over at the Poetry Foundation, Barr parrots Gioia's critique of academia, backing it up with some hands-on experience that may prove even more important than his familiarity with deregulation: Back in 1994, when serving as chairman of Bennington College's board of trustees, Barr drove through a plan to eliminate tenure at that institution and to fire two dozen full-time faculty members who had previously enjoyed its protection. The censure his actions brought upon the college from the American Association of University Professors seems neither to bother Barr nor to be remembered by those who profile him in the media. But as an example of his contempt for the professoriat, and as a taste of the designs he may have on academia, where a modicum of autonomy from market forces can still be found, the Bennington purge speaks volumes.

The deregulation of Bennington was carried out under the guise of fiscal necessity, but to lend it legitimacy a pedagogical "philosophy" was concocted as well. So while they crushed faculty governance structures, Barr and Co. also floated the slogan that instructors should henceforth "practice what they teach," meaning that non-creative types (art historians, for instance, as opposed to studio artists, or literary scholars who refrain from writing novels) were unproductive parasites who deserved their pink slips. A similar view informs Barr's take on the poetry world. In interviews, he speaks eagerly of the "hothouse" feel to much contemporary poetry, and of his desire to toss a brick through the glass. "There is great poetry being written in the academy," he told Kevin Larimer of *Poets & Writers*, "but we might get a broader experience base in poetry if people did things other than write and teach." Need a concrete example? Here is Barr's favorite: "Ernest Hemingway. In 1933 he took his first safari . . . he shot lions and went home and wrote about it. . . . I don't know a lot of poets who do that."

Poetics of the Backlash

The common project shared by Gioia at the NEA, Barr at the Poetry Foundation, and their partner in several recent projects, Ted Kooser, a former Nebraska insurance underwriter who became U.S. poet laureate in 2004, can be summarized rather simply: to deny, disrupt, and discredit existing networks of poetry production, which are seen as pathetically small, disgustingly smug, and—like subsidized farming—crypto-socialist, and to restore to his rightful place of preeminence the reader, referred to alternately as "common" or "general," who validates good poetry by actually paying for it on the open market and who never did have much use for the lin-

guistic shenanigans of modernism and its successors. As Barr puts it, "By growing the universe of readers who will buy books of poetry, the Foundation hopes to bring economic as well as artistic life to the business of writing poetry."

The assertion upon which the whole program rests—namely that poetry has somehow shrunk to become the exclusive property of the same latté-besotted, wind-surfing, advanced-degree-holding snobs who voted for Kerry—is a fabrication so flimsy as to border on hallucination. But the hallucination is expressive. What it says is that Gioia, Barr, and Kooser, not to mention the folks at the *Washington Times, The Weekly Standard*, and *The New Criterion* who celebrate the poetic regime change, all very much wish that the large and diverse audience for poetry that manifestly does exist today would *disappear*, so that it could be replaced with a more docile and homogeneous one of their own choosing.

Just imagine. Gone would be the many poets and readers of poetry who relished the explosive growth and democratization of the art in the sixties, a decade that rekindled the former alliance between poetry and social progress (after it had been smothered by, of all people, academics of the Cold War persuasion). Forgotten would be the mimeograph magazines, and the xerox ones and the web-based ones that followed, which irrevocably decentralized the world of poetry by taking the power of publication out of the hands of a few authoritative editors and presses and giving it directly to poets themselves, who often choose gift economies over profit-driven ones. All traces of the social movements that made such vigorous use of poetry to articulate their aspirations and their anger would be erased: gone the feminists, gone the gay writers and readers, gone the advocates of civil rights and multiculturalism. Gone, finally, and most satisfyingly, the cities—New York and Brooklyn, San Francisco and Berkeley, Chicago, Boston, Atlanta, Los Angeles, Detroit—unpredictable points of contact and collision that inspire vernacu-

lar poetries, cosmopolitan avant-garde poetries, and everything in between.

And what is the market force previously and unjustly neglected by the nation's literati, that vast untapped dynamo of poetic renewal envisioned by verse's self-appointed deregulators? Is it the barn and tractor set, as Kooser sometimes suggests? The recently bereaved or betrothed, desperate for a serviceable sentiment? The grandchildren of Nixon's silent majority, whose cravings for rhymed quatrains go unfulfilled? John Barr worries that "commuters, travelers in hotel rooms who would love to see an anthology at night, airplane travelers," are not getting their daily verse. The deepest desire of our businessmen poets, it seems, is for a twenty-first century poetry reader who has been resurrected directly from the nineteenth, a Rip van Winkle whose eyes open on the same page of Longfellow he'd been reading before dozing off, a sleeping beauty unacquainted with the temptations of Gertrude Stein.

And Deliver Us from Modernism

After a year of quiet deliberation and strategic planning, the Poetry Foundation began in the spring of 2005 to publicize the uses to which it will put Ruth Lilly's millions. Naturally, there will be a website. And henceforth poets will receive $6 a line rather than $2 for publishing in the redesigned pages of *Poetry*. Some new prizes have been concocted: one for a neglected master, one for humor, one for a slow starter who publishes his or her first volume after the age of fifty. Of course there will also be a poll—perhaps, more accurately, a market survey—to determine American attitudes toward poetry. (Barr predicted to the *New York Times* that it would be "a major reality check" that should "tell us exactly what's going on out there.")

Two collaborative projects are also underway, one with Poet Laureate Kooser, the other with "kindred spirit" Dana Gioia. Both projects express a yearning for the premodernist nineteenth century, when verse flourished in newspapers—as Kooser will strive to make it do again—and schoolchildren were force-fed poems for memorization and recitation—as Gioia wishes them again to do in national "recitation bees" judged on the four criteria of accuracy, eye contact, volume, and understanding of the poem.

Despite the sporadic, halfhearted attempts he makes to seem open to poetry's "exploratory" or experimental side, it is clear that what Barr loves best are poems he can "parse," poems that, as he puts it, "go from A to B to C" and continue "a tradition that has existed for hundreds of years" that he calls "the poetry of the rational or the didactic." So it is no surprise that these are just the kinds of poems that Kooser has good-naturedly offered to deliver in free weekly installments to editors of some forty thousand mid-sized and rural newspapers across the country, with a dedicated website built and operated by the Poetry Foundation for further dissemination of Kooser's "product."

In introducing his newspaper column, "American Life in Poetry," Kooser likes to emphasize the home states of the versifiers he has chosen: There are South Dakota poets and Kentucky poets and Minnesota poets and Nebraska poets and Ohio poets and Washington state poets and Illinois poets and Texas poets. And he tries to connect with his readership through earnest opening gambits like: "Perhaps your family passes on the names of loved ones to subsequent generations." He keeps the poems ultra brief and relentlessly "accessible," favoring inconspicuous free-verse narratives with one or two rhymed things thrown in for fun. It is never hard to "parse" them, true, but it is hard to imagine getting interested in or excited by them.

Here's how a glum four months of Kooser's column parses out: A speaker observes an alienated couple as they dourly squirt Windex at each other's faces from opposite sides of a pane they're cleaning. A speaker assists minimally in the burial of an acquaintance. A speaker recalls buying red shoes for a woman who hasn't been seen since. A speaker

feels remorse for having a crippled piglet put down. A speaker observes a neighbor hauling bales to his barn as autumn descends. A speaker employs end rhyme to convince himself to give up booze. Biting into a potato, a speaker recalls his impoverished childhood. A speaker is reminded by moonflowers of her recently deceased mother. A speaker contemplates an elderly veteran in a parade. A speaker celebrates the arrival of spring. A speaker looks on as a male peacock's ostentatious display fails to interest a female intent on food. A speaker named after his grandfather feels his forebear's presence while filling out forms and at supper. A tamed speaker recalls his youthful virility on the eve of his fortieth birthday. A speaker likens an elderly neighbor in a housecoat to a sunset. A speaker contemplates the life of an obsessive collector of Noah's Ark images and trinkets. A speaker likens love to salt.

Barr likes to say that "poetry's golden age will come when it is in front of a general audience." But no Midas could transform this meager stuff into good poetry. This is not because the poems Kooser selects are populist in intention. It is because they are almost entirely devoid of verbal wit, cognitive surprise, or strong passions. And if the businessmen poets think they will widen the market share for their products, perhaps it is time to reconsider just how much worldly savoir-faire they in fact possess: Such poems barely compete for attention with a paleolithic comic strip like "Beetle Bailey," let alone Def Poetry Jam or the latest Clear Channel megahit. As for literary competence, Barr admits: "I think that if I had been a subscriber to *Poetry* magazine in 1912, when it was founded, and Harriet Monroe picked poems by the unknown poets, T.S. Eliot, Ezra Pound, and others, I would not have understood them, and I wouldn't have known that they were to become known, a century later, as the great modern poets. I am a little bit humble about recognizing the next great talent when it shows up."

The next great talent in American poetry would be lucky *not* to be recognized by Barr and his friends at the NEA and Library of Congress, for there's no telling whether he or she would survive the attack this *novum*-phobic crew would no doubt launch in the name of rational didacticism and the beleaguered general reader. With hundreds of millions of private and federal dollars now at their disposal, the businessmen poets are positioned to administer serious damage to one of the liveliest, most democratic, and brilliantly articulate art forms in America. But it is doubtful that their curious amalgam of economic elitism, drowsy formalism, and right-wing populism will prove a match for the Whitmanesque tradition of radical democracy, fearless formal investigation, and do-it-yourself ingenuity that has produced most of the country's greatest poetry. While the Poetry Foundation prescribes its Prozac poems to reluctant readers, the wide-awake poetry of the present can be expected to be everywhere otherwise occupied. ■

THERE IS ALWAYS ANOTHER REVOLUTION

Behold thou art like a satellite that takes
control of the planet it was orbiting; like
dreams that rebel against sleep; like prisoners who take for themselves prisoners; like
the fields and factories that rise up against
the workers; like a God who takes his own
name in vain.

—*Joshua Schuster*

REQUIEM FOR A BUREAUCRAT

VICTOR G. REUTHER: JANUARY 1, 1912–JUNE 3, 2004

by Jim McNeill

O N JANUARY 11, 1937, two weeks into the epic sit-down strike at General Motors in Flint, Michigan, a young socialist named Victor Reuther arrived in a rickety sound car at GM's Fisher Body Plant No. 2. GM had just turned off the plant's heat—it was 16 degrees outside—and cut off food to the sit-down strikers inside. Reuther, seeking to lift the strikers' spirits, asked if they'd like to hear a song. "Can the music," they cried, "get us some food."

Young Reuther did as he was told. Quickly, he organized a group of pickets outside the plant to face down the company guards at its gates. Outnumbered, the guards retreated. The food was delivered, the strikers cheered. But suddenly, in squad cars and on foot, Flint's police force surged up the street. Firing tear-gas shells before them, the police scattered the pickets and seemed poised to rout the strikers inside.

It was the most desperate moment of the most important strike in American history. And at that moment, Reuther took to the microphone in his sound car and directed the counterattack. On his order, the strikers used makeshift slingshots to hurl heavy car-door hinges at the police; using the plant's fire hoses, they poured freezing water down on the officers. Though the police began firing bullets when they ran out of tear gas, the sit-down strikers held firm. It was the first and last attempt to remove the GM strikers by force.

When Reuther died two years ago at the age of ninety-two, all the obituaries highlighted his heroic role at Flint. Given the high drama, how could they not? And yet by focusing so heavily on Flint, by intimating that the rest of his long life was anticlimax, the obituaries obscured Reuther's real legacy. His most important contribution to history came not as a street fighter but as a bureaucrat.

Victor Reuther would hate being remembered as a bureaucrat. Given the term's standard usage, he'd have every right to. Usually we think of bureaucrats as staid Republicans or, at best, stolid Democrats. We think of them building corporations, not battling them. But Reuther and the United Auto Workers didn't tame the American auto industry in one furious battle at Flint. Rather, they did it through decades of painstaking labor, through the unavoidably tedious work of building a strong and sophisticated union; they did it, in other words, by building a bureaucracy.

Of course, the UAW was like no bureaucracy America had ever seen. Militant communists, committed socialists, and conservative Catholics all jostled for position in the union's early years. Factions allied with one another one month and warred against each other the next. Reuther, the grandson of a German pacifist and son of a West Virginia socialist, thrived in the union's political hothouse. Though only twenty-four when he began his work with the Auto Workers, Reuther was no political novice. In 1919, when he was seven years old, Victor's father took him and his older brother Walter—who would become the UAW's president—to visit Socialist Party leader Eugene Debs in prison. By the time Victor entered high school, his father was staging weekly political debates at home between the brothers. Those debates included another Reuther brother, Roy, who would go on to serve as the UAW's political director.

By 1932, Walter and Victor had moved to Detroit and become active in the Socialist Party. That summer, Roy joined them in Michigan and all three brothers campaigned across the state for the party's presidential candidate. Despite their best efforts, socialism's proud red banner fluttered weakly that fall—the party's standard-bearer won 2 percent of the vote in Michigan. Still, that 1932 drubbing offered the brothers another, more immediate opportunity. Soon after the election, Walter's political activities got him fired from his job at Ford. That prompted Victor to quit his classes at Detroit City College, and in early 1933 the two left the United States to take a decidedly political tour of Europe. In England, they met with Fabian aristocrats and hard-left factory hands; in Germany, they commiserated with students struggling against the newly ascendant Nazis; and finally, in the Soviet Union, they spent a year and a half helping to launch production at the massive Gorky Auto Works. While they were overseas, Roy threw himself into the fight to organize America's autoworkers. When Victor and Walter returned to the United States in 1935, they joined him in the defining crusade of their age.

～

For those of us fated to live on the American left, no decade excites the imagination like the thirties. Workers, prostrate as the Depression began, rose up against America's discredited business class; even the president felt compelled to denounce the nation's "economic royalists." In no other era has the left had so much influence in American life. Proletarian novels were written and actually read. Yes, the plots were predictable and the characters wooden, but in the thirties there was real truth in those stories of teeming masses triumphing in glorious strikes.

Of course, America's workers had won great labor battles before. In 1912, tens of thousands of textile workers in Lawrence, Massachusetts, famously demanded bread and roses, and briefly won both. But barely a year after that victorious strike, the mill owners had broken their union. The Lawrence strikers and the Wobblies who led them left behind some inspiring slogans but not much more.

Labor's great achievement in the thirties wasn't winning massive strikes, but consolidating the gains from those victories. Without the leadership of gifted organizers like the Reuthers, the members of the UAW and the decade's other fledgling unions would likely have suffered the same fate as Lawrence's mill hands. By the end of 1937, less than a year after the Flint strike, the U.S. economy had fallen back into the deepest trough of the Depression, and GM and many other manufacturers exploited the crisis to launch a counterattack against the fragile industrial unions. By the beginning of 1939, only 6 percent of the nation's GM workers were paying dues to the UAW. Of Flint's forty-two thousand GM workers, just five hundred were still UAW members in good standing—the same number as before the sit-down strike.

At that dark hour, Walter Reuther was picked to run the union's GM department. (Things were so desperate in the UAW that Victor, the hero of Flint, had been purged from the national union during a 1938 faction fight and hung on only as a volunteer organizer at a Detroit local.) Walter moved quickly to centralize the chaotic structure of the GM department. With the automaker refusing to recognize the UAW's authority in its plants, union leaders felt they had to strike. Yet Walter knew the Auto Workers didn't have the strength to sustain a companywide walkout. Instead, he convinced the union's remaining members to conduct a "strategy strike" against GM's tool-and-die plants in the summer of 1939. The company couldn't retool for the 1940 model year without those plants and capitulated after four weeks. Reuther's carefully conceived strike arguably saved the union.

After war broke out in Europe in 1939, all three Reuther brothers were appointed to defense production boards that the United States hastily established. Together with other labor leaders they used those bureaucratic posts to

win some measure of justice for wartime workers. But while unions agreed to no-strike pledges that curbed their power during the war, businesses won cost-plus contracts that garnered them record profits. Victor grew increasingly frustrated with the profit-minded executives he served with on the defense boards, and soon after the war he argued that unions should stop "wrestl[ing] with business and government for a larger share of scarcity under a system of 'free enterprise.'" Writing in late 1945 in the left-leaning magazine *Common Sense*, Victor said labor should press for new "forms of social ownership." He admitted that the idea was "political dynamite," but he believed that only such explosive thinking could "blast away the obstructions to economic abundance and insure the expansion of political democracy."

It's bracing to read those words now and realize they weren't written by the delusional leader of a small socialist sect, but by a key official of the nation's most important union. What distinguished Victor from America's sad sectarians was his ability to wed utopian dreams to practical plans. And so, even as Victor wrote those bold words, he went along with other UAW bureaucrats in their decision to discipline rank-and-file members who'd been holding unauthorized strikes. Victor didn't deny that the wildcat strikers had legitimate grievances, but he feared that their unplanned strikes would bankrupt the UAW and leave it unable to take on the Big Three in postwar contract talks.

Though the UAW ultimately fell short of achieving Victor's social democratic dreams, we shouldn't minimize the union's postwar achievements. The UAW doubled the wages of American autoworkers in less than a generation, and did it in the face of brutal opposition. In 1948, Walter, then the president of the union, was shot and almost killed in his home. A year later, in a nearly identical attack, Victor almost lost his life and did lose his right eye. Though the evidence implicated mobsters with ties to Ford's former security chief, FBI director J. Edgar Hoover blocked an investigation and the shooters were never prosecuted. Despite the attacks, the Reuthers continued with their work. Shortly before the attempt on his life, Victor had spent time in Europe spreading the gospel of industrial democracy. After recovering from the shooting, Victor went back. As the journalist Murray Kempton wrote, he worked as an "organizer not out for dues but to help restore the soul of European labor."

Victor returned to the United States in 1953. Though he served in Washington as the director of the UAW's international affairs department, he also advised Walter on domestic politics, and the two of them never stopped searching for ways to push America leftward. In 1961, Victor made time to meet with a University of Michigan undergraduate who led a tiny campus group called Students for a Democratic Society. After the meeting, Victor convinced the union to give $10,000 to SDS. A year later, SDS leaders would gather at a UAW summer camp in Port Huron, Michigan, to draft their famous manifesto—and another decade of left-wing ferent was launched.

Victor and the union were even more vitally involved in the civil rights movement. In the debate leading up to the passage of the 1964 Civil Rights Act, Victor and other UAW officials frequently set aside their union work to lobby full-time for the bill. In 1963, the Auto Workers gave more than $100,000 to Martin Luther King Jr.'s Southern Christian Leadership Conference to help it prepare for the March on Washington. More than five thousand Auto Workers attended the march, the largest delegation from any group.

~

There's a classic picture of the Reuther brothers taken at the UAW convention in 1937, just as they were emerging as leaders of the union. Victor, the youngest and tallest of the three, stands between Walter and Roy, both of whom sport broad, toothy grins. Victor's lips, by contrast, are set in a wry smile. The older brothers have the look of eager warriors totally focused on the floor fights to come. But Victor's heavy-lidded eyes seem to see something a little further in the distance. Even after his right eye was shot out, Victor's vision always seemed a little stronger than anyone else's in labor.

What made Victor so special—what made him the exemplary labor bureaucrat—was his ability to see, as Walter sometimes didn't, that unions themselves aren't sacred, only their mission is. Walter built the UAW into a powerful economic engine for workers during his twenty-four years as president, but under him the union's internal politics became rather machine-like, too. Though Walter tolerated no corruption, neither did he allow much dissent. Victor was one of the few people in the UAW who could challenge his brother's thinking. Tragically, on the most disastrous issue of their time, the Vietnam War, Victor was unable to change it. Walter had strong reservations about the war, but he suppressed them and hoped that by maintaining his close ties to LBJ he could press for more liberal domestic policies. Instead, as Victor feared, the war shattered the liberal coalition the UAW had done so much to build, and the nation began its decades-long drift to the right. After Walter died in a 1970 plane crash, the founding generation of the union soldiered on for a few more years. But as they retired—Victor left in 1972—the

union began to falter. By the eighties the Auto Workers were accepting one round of concessionary contracts after another. Today, the union's leaders stare into the abyss and find the hapless executives of GM and Delphi staring back at them.

One can regard the UAW's decline as proof of the pitiless theories of Robert Michels, the German sociologist who argued early in the twentieth century that every organization, no matter how democratic at birth, assumes an oligarchic form as it matures. Michels' "Iron Law of Oligarchy"—divined largely from his study of the German labor movement—described how even young revolutionary leaders "end by fusing with the old dominant class" they set out to topple. "It is probable," Michels mourned, "that this cruel game will continue without end."

But Victor refused to play by the rules of that game. Ten years into his retirement, when a group of dissidents challenged the UAW's ossified leadership, Victor made the astonishing decision to go back to the barricades and join the reformers. Though Victor and his allies didn't prevail against the UAW hierarchy, they did set loose a reform wave that continues to shape the labor movement to this day. Victor worked with the insurgents who brought democracy to the Teamsters union in the early nineties, and that victory made it possible to unseat the conservative leadership of the AFL-CIO in 1995. Sadly, the progressives who replaced them have had no better luck in reversing labor's decline. But now the labor movement is undergoing an even more searching round of reform. Let us hope that the latest wave of reformers are inspired by Victor's example. Let's hope they can match the soaring rhetoric of that young socialist in the sound car at Flint. And when today's workers cry out for food, let's hope that today's reformers, like young Victor, have a plan to deliver it. ∎

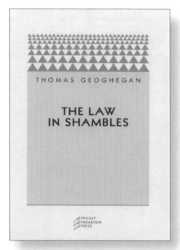
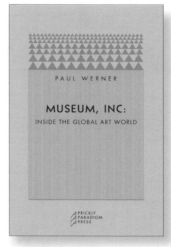

From THE RING OF STRATEGIC INFLUENCE

It's sometimes valuable from a military standpoint
to be able to engage in deception. (Dick Cheney)

TRANSLATIONS PART
predawn vertical insertion for invasion
unlawful or arbitrary deprivation of life for killing
"You always write it's bombing, bombing, bombing. It's not bombing, it's air support."
target servicing for putting artillery fire on target
permanent pre-hostility for peace
In 1947 the Department of War was renamed the Department of Defense because when the
war is "over" it's difficult to ask for an increase in the war budget.
damage limitation for offensive strikes
soft targets for cities where people live
kinetic energy penetrators for bullets
violence processing for combat
national security has no definition and therefore cannot be translated.

KNOW YOUR TARGET
remove any trace of the color red
show soldiers with chin beards rather than clean-shaven faces
don't use thought bubbles; they're confusing
add bananas to a bowl of fruit

keep in mind that the target is suspicious
and will look for hidden unfavorable meanings
insure that only one interpretation,
the intended one, can be given each sentence.
do not leave any thoughts for the target to fill in

caption everything

NATURE PART
there are leaves in leaflets
updrafts and down drafts
follow the general direction of the wind
constant pull of gravity
modified wing pods
detaching the fins
winds, tides, currents
sounds projected over water
low-lying coastal plains
William Carlos Williams compares a young housewife to a fallen leaf
and then runs her over
but what about the leaflet?
a beehive is direct fire with steel dart fleshettes
helicopter birds in the elephant grass
my green eye sees at night, laying chilly for a mad minute
where are the white mice this time?
At ten a.m. the young leaflet
moves about in updrafts and down drafts behind
the walls of her target-rich environment.
I pass solitary in my car.

—*Jena Osman*

ONCE MORE, WITH ACTORS

THE CHAUTAUQUA REVISITED

by Matt Weiland

I AM AN AMERICAN, Midwestern-born, and I have gone at American things. I have skinnydipped and snowmobiled, bowled with others and bowled alone. I know the lyrics to "It's a Small World" by heart; I brighten at the sound of bat hitting ball; I have been known to frequent parades. But if Teddy Roosevelt was right when he declared the chautauqua to be "the most American thing in America," I confess I've been too long a stranger in my own land. How many times have I seen this strange word, puzzled over references to the great cultural movement it signified, and yet troubled myself so little to discover its meaning. The chautauqua may be as deep in the American grain as door-to-door salesmen and Sunday football, but to me it's always been as much a relic of bygone America as the bison.

So, when I heard that chautauqua was being revived in the midst of the great American heartland, my patriotic duty was clear: I had to set out for the Midwestern prairie to stalk this great buffalo of the American mind.

∼

There's nothing better than a lazy summer evening spent with chinking ice under a canvas tent—I mean the circus kind, the billowing striped affair that says *summertime!* and reeks of high-rent clowns or holy matrimony—except when it's hot and mosquitoes are out in force and the drinks truck is cashed out and the tent guys you watched assemble the tent didn't seem sure where to put the poles in. Tonight in western Illinois it's nearly ninety-five degrees and there's no breeze and the chair is as hard as pavement

and the poles are leaning and creaking and making to fall; plus I'm waiting for Coco Chanel, the first speaker I've come to see at the weeklong Heartland Chautauqua.

A century ago, traveling chautauquas—"peripatetic cultural circuses," one historian called them—began a generation's run as the most popular entertainment of the age. Back then, I could have spent a summer's week with several thousand other people listening to high-minded lectures by muckrakers and novelists, scientists and seekers, all accompanied by a steady stream of light music and entertainments under a big canvas tent. These days, in the variant revived under the auspices of the National Endowment for the Humanities, the tents are back, the crowds are returning, and the music is as schmaltzy as ever. But whereas in the original chautauqua the crowds enjoyed the oratory of the foremost minds of their time, the crowds today look on in bemusement as teachers and actors dressed as popular figures from history deliver monologues in character. Tonight, a three-piece band called No Reason has just finished belting out some Crosby, Stills & Nash covers, and Coco Chanel is due onstage any minute.

I've taken an aisle seat in the back of the big striped tent—the art of emergency lecture-hall escapes dies hard—and am waiting for the interminable pre-event gratitude to be expressed to everyone's content. The organizer, earnest and bluff, thanks a long list of major corporations for their support, then thanks another long list of local businessmen whom everyone else seems to know personally and who seem to have given their life fortunes or lungs to make Heartland Chautauqua happen this year. Finally, the emcee pauses and looks out at us—there are about sixty people in the audience, but I'm pretty sure he's looking directly at me—and speaks the dread words: "So come with me now, as we go back in history, to a time when. . . ." I have a feeling I remember from the first day of class—*must leave now*—but to my left, blocking the aisle, is a tangle of wide women who won't take their seats. There will be no easy escape.

When I turn back to the stage, the organizer is gone and the lights are low. There's a whoosh in the crowd, necks craning as Coco enters the tent behind us and swishes up to the stage. We're all silent now, and even the rambunctious teens in back seem resigned to sticking it out. It's somehow getting hotter as the sun begins to set, and Coco has not been to this part of Illinois before: She is overdressed and sweating profusely and seems about to faint. She adjusts the microphone and looks out at us. Here, in the Illinois heat, this thoughtful, kindly woman is about to humiliate herself—and us—by acting out some fantasy. It's like watching a middle-aged mortgage banker or contractor win a pregame trip to the pitcher's mound of his favorite ballpark. Lumbering out of the crowd in tasseled loafers and polo shirt, he is still the authoritative man behind a desk who denies your loan application or installs your

patio deck; a moment later, huffing up on the mound, he is reduced to middle youth, the time of wide-eyed love for plastic infantrymen and sweet soda pop and brightly colored bags of chips. Up there on the stage this woman of grace and gravitas, this respected holder of advanced degrees, is going to bomb. And I am embarrassed for her and for me and for all of us.

⁓

"There was no public lecture till Emerson made it," Bronson Alcott said. Emerson was stiff on stage and often hard to understand, but his lectures were a national phenomenon in the middle of the nineteenth century. In a journal entry from 1839, soon after he took to the stage, Emerson declared the public lecture to be "a new literature, which leaves aside all tradition, time, place, circumstances, and addresses an assembly as mere human beings, no more." He went on to deliver as many as fifteen hundred lectures in the subsequent forty years, crossing the country to present his ideas in public, as one mere human being to another.

The chautauquas grew from these roots. Schooled on Emerson's lectures, inspired by the rising tide of mass education after the Civil War, and fueled by a radical faith in the democratic spirit, Lewis Miller, an Akron machine-tool manufacturer already famed for his Buckeye Mower and Reaper, and the Rev. John Heyl Vincent, a prominent Methodist minister, established what would become the chautauqua in 1874. They transformed a former Methodist meeting site near a lake in western New York into a grand training institute for Sunday school teachers. (Some say the local Indians called the lake "Bag Tied in the Middle," or Chautauqua.)

Emersonian to the core, Miller and Vincent believed in self-improvement for its own sake, an uplift untarnished by personal advancement or private profit. As Vincent wrote, they hoped to "educate the people, and all the people—the poorest and meanest of them—until in lordly way, worthy of royal blood, they refuse to be trodden upon or ordered about."

Miller and Vincent's plans were a success from the start. Audiences virtually tripled in each of the first few years, and the Chautauqua Assembly expanded from two weeks to eight and from a local affair into a regional, and finally, national movement. Political leaders swiftly realized the opportunities Chautauqua's platform presented. In 1876, President Ulysses S. Grant steamboated in, and in 1880 presidential candidate James A. Garfield declared, "It has been the struggle of the world to get more leisure, but it was left for Chautauqua to show how to use it." By the 1880s, Chautauqua was the chief symbol and main exponent of the idea of popular education for all.

But it was the institution's next twenty-five years that would leave its lasting legacy: the tradition of traveling or "circuit" chautauqua. Midwestern entrepreneurs, the 100 percent Americans so familiar from Sinclair Lewis's acid portraits and Sherwood Anderson's bitter tales, formed centralized firms in Chicago, Kansas City, and Cedar Rapids to organize chautauqua circuits: A group of speakers and entertainers would be booked, a week of chautauqua would be offered to towns along the route of a major railroad, and the chautauquans would "morally roll along," as one participant put it, from one town to the next throughout the summer.

The firms appealed to the civic pride and nose for profit of each town's leading businessmen to guarantee advance subscriptions and thereby ensure the chautauqua's presence the following summer. Once a chautauqua was booked and the happy day approached, Main Street's finest would naturally cajole their neighbors and friends into attending.

The week would then feature a mix of educational and inspirational lecturers leavened by light entertainers and musicians. There were preachers, explorers, scientists, and statesmen; glee clubs, accordionists, and bell ringers; elocutionists, novelists, yodelers, and whistlers. One participant described them as "the greatest aggregation of performers the world has ever known."

Soon what was known as the "chautauqua belt" spread across the Midwest, as a core of about thirty chautauqua towns in 1904 grew to at least ten thousand in 1921. By 1923,

> **Chautauqua's careful dodging of the present makes its tent a canvas cage, a bubble in which to hide from the light and heat of the world. It is one thing to hear Bob La Follette assail the trusts and another to hear "Bob La Follette" talk about how he used to assail the trusts.**

circuit chautauqua was perhaps the most popular form of public entertainment in the country, with 10 million people buying tickets and as many as 35 million paying admission. "Our year is made up of fifty-one weeks of humdrum slavery," wrote one South Dakota farmer's wife, "and one week of chautauqua." The following year, the height of circuit chautauqua's glory, the editor of *The New Republic* declared:

> [N]owhere else under the quiet stars of this moment will you find a more characteristic expression of the American idea.

~

When I ask the organizer of the present-day Heartland Chautauqua why they've chosen to come to Monmouth, Illinois, she says there is a great tradition of chautauqua in the area, and she shows me a photograph of a circuit chautauqua held in Monmouth in 1911: striped tents amid the trees; neckties and boaters and flouncing skirts everywhere. But she doesn't know much else about it, so I head to the Galesburg Public Library, a half hour west of here, to see what I can find out.

In Galesburg, the librarian tells me that there were chautauquas in Monmouth, but the big ones were right here in Galesburg, with its Burlington Northern railroad station and distinguished Knox College in town. After a little searching, she hands me a manila folder stuffed with programs from the Galesburg chautauquas of 1898 to 1902. That first year, 1898, the chautauqua tent out by Rice Lake held 2,500 people.

I'm staring at the 1899 program, regretting that I've come a century late to hear the Hon. A. Spencer Zook on "Known and Unknown Quantities," Col. H. W. J. Ham on "The Snollygoster in Politics," and the Rev. Lewis L. Thomas on "Saloonism versus God," when an old man walks up to the reference desk to ask a question of the librarian's young deputy, a prim and proper girl who seems finished with a year or two at Galesburg High School.

"Ma'am, excuse me," he says. "Excuse me, but can you help me find out how to spell *shillelagh?*"

The deputy is nonplussed. "Shillelagh?"

"Yeah, shillelagh, you know, an old walking stick. I used the word the other day in the grocery store. It's a kind of stick. I said to a woman there, who was walking with a cane, Boy, you've got a big shillelagh. She said, Why, I never thought of that. It's a kind of stick."

The deputy pulls down a Webster's, riffles through to S and, her finger in the page, reads out how to spell *shillelagh* to the man. He says thank you and heads out.

The Heartland folks have set up their tent on the campus of Monmouth College, and by early evening the audience starts to arrive. You know them already: They are familiar from a continuous tape-loop of TV features on the run-up to the Iowa Caucus or the aftermath of a Missouri heat wave; it's a kind of fantasy audience for publishers of anchorman memoirs and organizers of ice cream socials—a lot of silent, crease-faced men in wind-

breakers and baseball hats advertising farm machinery and aircraft carriers, led about by kindly women with strong arms and an air of impatience. It is the same crowd, if older and less formally dressed, that the circuit chautauqua drew a century ago.

Today the Heartland Chautauqua's theme is the Roaring Twenties. Besides Coco Chanel, they've lined up an eclectic mix of twenties icons: the rising young Missouri politician Harry Truman; the liberalizing first pastor of Riverside Church in New York, the Rev. Harry Emerson Fosdick; and the Kalamazoo novelist Edna Ferber, flush with the success of *Show Boat* and *So Big* (for which she won the Pulitzer Prize in 1924). But tonight belongs to Henry Ford. A larger crowd is here than turned out for Coco, and I'm in an aisle seat in the back again as Henry Ford makes his way to the stage.

Playing Henry Ford is Doug Mishler, a typical modern chautauquan. He's got a PhD in American cultural history, he tells a story with vigor and charm, and he wears a wig well. Like virtually all the other chautauquans I talk to, he loves chautauqua, he's been doing it for years, and he has played a variety of characters—P.T. Barnum, Theodore Roosevelt, and William Lloyd Garrison, among others.

Henry Ford tells a joke as soon as he grabs the microphone. "You all know what the UAW-CIO stands for, don't you? Well don't you? Why, it stands for U Are Working—Cut It Out!" The men in the audience laugh heartily and break into applause. It's hard to tell whether there's any irony about the laughter or whether the audience is just as inclined

to bust a union as Henry Ford was. Perhaps it's not surprising; this is, after all, a performance put on by an organization with an air-quotes view of history: Its website claims that Heartland Chautauqua is a "revival of that old feeling of excitement when people would spend a week in the summer going to the big tent to hear 'William Jennings Bryan' or 'Andrew Carnegie' give a lecture."

The bulk of Henry Ford's talk is standard stuff: a straightforward if artful recitation of life achievements and world events. He recounts the introduction of the Model T and mass production and his views on the First World War. It's a live-action Ken Burns documentary right there in front of us, informative and easy to swallow, without the endless slow pans or ubiquitous PBS logo in the corner. Eventually Henry Ford utters his famous line: "History is bunk." Here we are, a couple hundred of us under a tent on a lovely summer's night, listening to the past—and the past is mocking us.

The performance ends, and I brace for the questions. Part of the standard drill at chautauquas now is a section at the end in which the performer answers questions from the audience while still in character. The audience tends to address the performer in character, too, which the organizers seem to like. "Mr. Ford," someone asks, "what was the source of your anti-Semitism?" Henry Ford gives a long answer, neither dodging the issue nor simplifying it. "Mr. Ford," someone else asks, "did your views on history ever change?" Henry Ford says he meant his infamous remark as a kind of hymn to innovation, to creative destruction of the old in order to forge the new. I bristle, suspecting he's about to break into an anachronous paean to the Pursuit of Wow or some other management piety of the recent past. But Henry Ford ventures the guess that many in the future will misquote him, or take his comment out of context, so he reads out the full, original quote:

> History is more or less bunk. It's tradition. We don't want tradition. We want to live in the present, and the only history that is worth a tinker's damn is the history we make today.

Henry Ford has wandered into an interesting thicket of American thought here, the debate over the "usable past" inaugurated by the chautauqua-era critic Van Wyck Brooks. One need not even leave the confines of Galesburg itself to be reminded how deep this line of thinking runs in American life. At the Carl Sandburg State Historic site in Galesburg, the backyard garden of Sandburg's boyhood home is filled with paving stones engraved with lines from his poems, including a fragment from his 1918 poem "Prairie":

> I speak of new cities and new people.
> I tell you the past is a bucket of ashes.
> I tell you yesterday is a wind gone down,
>   a sun dropped in the west.
> I tell you there is nothing in the world,
>   only an ocean of to-morrows
>   a sky of to-morrows.

Surely there's a difference between Ford's past and Sandburg's—and especially between the present that the socialist poet and the anti-Semitic auto titan would use their pasts for. But I find myself chewing on bunk and ashes as the next few questions come and go. Why was I inclined to mock the wigged man? The organizers, it turns out, have hired exactly the right chautauquan, one who says things worth disagreeing with, and I suspect that they have pledged a chicken dinner to any audience member who asks a tough question besides. But then comes a voice from the back: "Mr. Ford," says a man in a visor and white polo shirt, "I'm a little concerned about how the rumble seat came about. Can you tell us about that?"

~

The circuit chautauqua became a kind of pulpit for progress in the years before the First World War, responsible in part for the rapid spread of public support for social reform. "In the tents," wrote Merle Curti in *The Growth of American Thought*, "Jane Addams made Hull House live in the minds of rural folk . . . and Samuel Gompers publicized the aims of the 'organized toilers.' "

The chautauqua circuit routinely featured these and such other social reformers and muckrakers as Jacob Riis, Lincoln Steffens, Eugene Debs, Booker T. Washington, and Robert La Follette. Ida Tarbell, author of a famous series of essays exposing the practices of Rockefeller's Standard Oil Company, not only went on the circuit, but edited *The Chautauquan* for years. Still, she was dubious at first:

> Scoffing Eastern friends told me that there would be bell ringers, trained dogs, and Tyrolese yodelers. I found no such entertainment, but I could hardly have fallen in with pleasanter company. . . . I saw at once that what I had joined was not, as I had hastily imagined, a haphazard semi-business, semi-philanthropic, happy-go-lucky new kind of barnstorming. It was serious work.

In 1908, the *Indianapolis News* sent a reporter with the chautauquas through Indiana, Iowa, Kansas, and Missouri. As doubtful as Tarbell and as inclined to scoff as her Eastern friends, the reporter was soon sending back glowing reports of La Follette's platform tirades against railroad barons, of the success of reformers in the face of "standpatters," and of the "rising political power of the chautauqua, from which platform the exponents of progressivism thunder their messages."

The most famous and crowd-pleasing circuit chautauquan of them all was William Jennings Bryan, "good for forty acres of parked Fords, any time, anywhere." Bryan hailed the chautauquas as a powerful force for molding public opinion, and he delivered thousands of lectures from circuit chautauqua stages. "People went to a chautauqua to be stimulated," wrote another historian. He meant more than just amusement:

> They saw their neighbors there. They watched the color creep up the neck of the local banker when Debs castigated the financial interests, and they planned to be present when the banker got his next shave from the barber, an unreconstructed Populist. If Debs had spoken at a political rally, the banker would not have gone, and there would have been no argument to anticipate. But everyone went to chautauqua.

But others saw in chautauqua nothing but the cheap uplift of Methodist ministers and second-rate minds. Ever vigilant against the booboisie, H.L. Mencken railed against circuit chautauqua's "bombastic trivialities"—its small-mindedness, its sappy moralism and, not least of all, the insistent use of its platform to proselytize for Prohibition (Carry Nation and Billy Sunday were regulars of the chautauqua stage, too). In his classic 1917 essay "The Sahara of the Bozart," Mencken blasted the chautauquas as the "idiotic certainties of ignorant men." And in 1924, Bruce Bliven summarized the opposition's view of chautauqua as "a mediocre enterprise which gives to dull, starved minds the meretricious sustenance they crave."

As other forms of public entertainment—the radio, the movies, and then television—eclipsed chautauqua's audience and renown through the middle of the century, Mencken's scoffing view is the one that stuck, and it reached me almost undiluted a half-century later.

⁓

Still unsure whether chautauqua is buncombe or better, I've come three hundred miles due east (and a century farther in time) to see an Indian chief, a frontiersman, and Johnny Appleseed. They're all here for a chautauqua in the tiny village of Archbold, Ohio. Archbold bills itself as "On Your Way to Just About Anywhere"—Interstate 80 runs only a few miles north of here—but everybody knows this is nowhere.

A giant green tent is billowing on the grounds of Historical Sauder Village, a cultural landmark in the area. In fact it's the only landmark in the area—the solitary red square for miles on Rand McNally's atlas. Historical Sauder Village was created by Erie J. Sauder, a descendent of the original Mennonite settlers. A former employee of a woodworking company and an expert whittler on the side, Sauder started his own company in 1934 to design and mass-produce ready-to-assemble furniture. Today, Archbold is home to a $500 million company that bears his name, with more than three thousand workers and 5 million square feet of factories. It churns out "oak-style" desks and furniture that anyone who's been to college or camp or a convalescent home would recognize.

Sauder himself retained his youthful reverence for the handmade. In 1976 he created Historical Sauder Village, a kind of Colonial Williamsburg on the prairie that is filled with ersatz shops demonstrating the fine art of printing or basketweaving or, the common currency of all heritage sites everywhere, candlemaking. In its rustic lanes and quaint buildings, special events are scheduled to fill in the time between chautauqua performances. There's an old-time fiddling contest, demonstrations of traditional arts and crafts, an ice cream social, and a barbershop quartet in full regalia. I spend the better part of my first morning watching a man make a broom.

The best count I can come up with suggests there are more than a thousand people here for the chautauqua. It's a state fair kind of crowd, with lots of jostling and waiting in lines and calling out for lost children. The organizers are stunned, grateful, impressed. "I just don't know what to tell you, I'm just flabbergasted," one tells me. "We weren't expecting this. Guess we sure know how to turn out." The Ohioans seem pleased with themselves, like they've brought the best dish to the potluck, but they're also anxious to get on with it.

When evening comes, seats are in short supply. Finally I find one—uncomfortably close to the stage. I coast through the first performance, a tall frontiersman, armed and in fringe. He gives a relentlessly balanced view of historical conflict between settlers and Indians. It's a largely colorless affair and I grow bored. I'm distracted, too, by the Mennonite families filling many of the center rows. What are they doing here? There are still many Amish and Mennonites living in this part of the Midwest; in fact, Ohio has the largest Amish community in the world—perhaps as many as fifty thousand live here. But I'm surprised a group of people that so adamantly rejects its neighbors' view of the present would subject itself to its neighbors' view of the past.

At the first few performances, all the questions are about lost knowledge. Both the kids and the adults want to know about the arts of daily life past: how to ride a horse, how to hunt for squirrels, how to find a swimming hole. The chautauquans gamely give them their due: The settler's wife demonstrates the proper use of her apron to bring in garden gatherings; the Indian shows how to cleanly and swiftly scalp a settler's wife. There's color here, and not just local. It's a vast, open-air seminar in pioneer social history.

I'm into it; I'm learning something; I stay. But toward the end I head off to search for the Mennonites. I can see them up ahead, but I am stuck in a crush of people as the Q-and-A session ends and the audience begins to file out. Next to me is an older couple from Napoleon, twelve miles south of here. I ask them why they've come. "It's about history, and we like that," says the husband, who sells used farm equipment. "Business is good—too good," he says when I ask him about it. "I end up selling off all my friends' and neighbors' stuff." He says he should have gotten out years ago. His wife is a teacher and she's on the board of the local library. "We used to have things like this when we were kids, but there hasn't been anything like it here in a long time." I talk with a middle-aged man from Defiance who sells insurance. "I've lived here my whole life," he says re-

peatedly. Defiance was a prominent stop on
the chautauqua circuit in the early years of
the twentieth century. William Jennings
Bryan gave his "Flower of the Flock" speech
there in 1911, and Booker T. Washington
came through the following year. But the
amphitheater was destroyed in a massive
flood in 1913, and Archbold is the closest
chautauqua has come since then. I ask him
what he makes of it all and he says, well, he's
lived here his whole life and the closest thing
to it he can remember is the Freedom Train,
which stopped in Archbold during its Bicen-
tennial-year haul from coast to coast. "It traveled all across the country," he tells me,

> and it carried with it the ruby slippers from *The
> Wizard of Oz* and all the trophies from the Major
> League World Series, just awesome things that
> never come to our part of the country. Archbold
> got to host that, and this Chautauqua reminds
> me so much of it because the community just
> pours out to support the thing.

I look up for the Mennonites, but they are
gone.

The next morning in Historical Sauder
Village I watch two ten-year-old boys in
nineteenth century garb demonstrate the
proper way to play that game with the hoop
and stick. My hoop careens off toward the
chickens. The kids patiently explain the
proper technique to me again, and for a third
time. A couple more swats and scared chickens and I give up to go see how rope is made.
Here an older kid tells a younger one to hold

the rope-making tool, and then they do a
hop-footed dance that makes rope appear in
the older kid's hand. I say, "Hot damn!" and
the older kid gives me a look. When I ask
him whether he's going to be a professional
rope maker when he grows up, he says, "No,
it's just good to know."

At last the sun begins to slide away and I
head back to the big tent. It is packed with
people, everyone is here, and it's impossible to
find a seat. The organizers are saying, "I know
it, I know it, isn't it just amazing?" The crowd
is buzzing. The Mennonites are back, all up in
the front, and I'm left standing on the far right
of the stage. It is Johnny Appleseed night.

Hank Fincken is playing Johnny Appleseed
at seventy years old, in 1854. From the moment he springs onstage it's obvious Fincken
is a trained actor. His face contorts in mock
rage or delight; his voice booms and whines
and hides; his phrasing is sharp on the
laughs, and when it's not he follows up with
a self-mocking refrain. He is a performer, a
good one, and he's got the crowd with him.

But this is not children's theater or library
story time; this Johnny Appleseed has no pot
on his head. In the course of less than an
hour, he outlines the troubled relations between Midwestern settlers, Indians, and the
English during the War of 1812—and he's
got a stick in for everyone. Johnny Appleseed
explains to us the differences between various
sorts of apples, demonstrates how to graft an

apple tree and properly plant a seed, and reveals which apples grew here in the corner of Ohio and why. Then he explains the process by which pioneers establish a claim to land, describes the travails of prairie settlers, and defends vegetarianism. He spends his remaining time detailing the ideas of Emanuel Swedenborg, the nineteenth century mystic, to which he subscribes.

When it's over I wade through the long applause to talk to Fincken. I wait as lines of fans come to greet him and get an autograph, and when at last we talk, we are the last ones there, more than an hour after the performance, and Historical Sauder Village staff in petticoats and bonnets are imploring us to leave so they can dismantle the benches and remove the bunting.

Fincken says he tries to capture the contradiction in the character of John Chapman (he insists on referring to Johnny Appleseed by his real name). He presents Chapman and his role on the Ohio frontier, he says, as a kind of lesson in prairie religiosity and practical education, staying sensitive to the complexities of history even as he strives to make Chapman dramatically appealing.

"The hard part," he says, "is do I present the character in terms of our values today, or do I present him in terms of his values then?" Fincken points out that another character he sometimes plays, a California gold miner circa 1849, was as contemptuous of the local Indians as any of his fellow miners, but he proposed paying them a fee to use their land. "In today's world," Fincken says, "he would be considered a kind of Indian-hater, but in his time he was considered very much a liberal!"

He's right, but I'm still not convinced he couldn't just give a lecture; why must he dress up and speak in character? Fincken claims that performance gives him and the audience a chance to see into the character more closely, more intensely, than would a traditional lecture. But isn't that just an excuse for second-rate, television-style dramatic reconstruction?

"No," he says. "People get tired of that slick stuff. Look, TV has invaded every place we have. This is not TV—the show you saw cannot be redone exactly. Of course we'd be lying if we said we recaptured history, but we give a good solid glimpse of the past, and that glimpse is how we came to be."

Sitting outside the tent, the sun going down, the Sauder Village maidens now exhorting us to leave, I am not sure. Wasn't this just another example of how we treat the past as just so much retro plunder? How we treat the past like some aging boar, removing its fangs and helping it up the steps to Disney's stage? Still, I was sorry it was over, and was mulling whether I could manage to graft an apple tree in my own backyard.

~

Some say the demise of the railroads killed off the chautauqua circuit, others that radio and the movies dealt the mortal blow. But all agree that by the late twenties the circuit was dominated by sappy emotionalizers, charlatans, and inspirational speakers; that the chautauqua movement, as one historian wrote, "was drowned in a flood of pap."

Most of the talks I saw in Illinois and Ohio proved that the flood has not yet subsided. They were historical melodramas or personal accounts of achievement, an approach to history cribbed from *Behind the Music* reruns and motivational infomercials. *I was born, I overcame hurdles, I emerged victorious. You can, too.* A far cry from starchy Victorian self-improvement; it is self-help at its soggiest.

And chautauqua's careful dodging of the American present makes its tent a canvas cage, a bubble in which to hide from the light and heat of the world. It is one thing to hear Bob La Follette assail the trusts and another to hear "Bob La Follette" talk about how he used to assail the trusts. The original chautauqua circuit, for all of its flaws, was about the American Now, with all its thorns and roses; today's revived version has nothing but dead flowers to show.

Lewis Mumford once wrote that what Emerson aimed for was "intellectual, or cultural, nakedness: the virtue of getting beyond the institution, the habit, the ritual, and finding out what it means afresh in one's own consciousness." The revived chautauqua will not restore the lecture's pride of place in public life, and though there may be a "Ralph Waldo Emerson" or two among its costumed speakers, there are no Emersons there.

Still, in some of the talks I could detect a trace of the old spirit of betterment for its own sake, of the noble nineteenth century movement to offer education to all—the same spirit that animated Carnegie's campaign for public libraries. Like a library's stacks, chautauqua is full of the dusty, the moldy, and the second-rate. But also like those stacks, it is a place to browse and wander, and among the happy sleepers out there in the crowd, I kept thinking that there might be someone, someone nobody knows, having the experience Richard Wright described in *Black Boy*—the moment out of the sun, the epiphany of the library card. ■

THE NATIONAL
HIGHWAY DEFENSE FUND

by *Whitney Terrell*

MY FATHER HAD LEFT KANSAS CITY after he finished high school. He'd joined the Navy in '44, learned to operate destroyer guns, and then shipped quietly off to watch the Japanese surrender in Tokyo Bay. He'd been on leave, visiting a shipmate in Asheville, North Carolina, when he met my mother, who at the time was seventeen but said that she was twenty-two and a graduate of Sarah Lawrence University. They were introduced on the back terrace of a piney country club, tucked into the shadow of the Blue Hills, because my father was claiming he'd gone to Boston U. They lied contiguously. "I'd seen him tee off that afternoon," my mother said metaphorically, "and here was this blond man—twice the size of all the men he was playing with—who hit this enormous drive. And it went perfectly straight up, as high as you could imagine, with a cute little draw at the end." There was no ceremony. My mother (her name was Alabaster Mann) was due in senior year social studies at Carl Sandburg high school in Hendersonville that fall. She was five foot even, wore her hair cut short and parted to the side, and when she quit Asheville with my father, she left behind her cheerleading skirt, her bathing cap, and that spring's yearbook. Her father, a traffic engineer in Hendersonville, retrieved these things in grief.

"I know I'm going to be something," her new husband had told her, driving, his fingers gripping the wheel. "I know I got it in me to do *something* great, make a mark someplace. All I ask is you be patient with me till I find out what it is."

By the summer of 1954, my father's great-ness still remained a phantom, believed in by no one but my mother and me. We were back in Kansas City then, where my father was hunting for work and spending his evenings on our apartment's white-columned porch, thumbing through biographies. "Look at this," he said, reading simultaneously from *The Story of a Fortune* and *The Last Billionaire*. "Jay Gould, at age twenty-four, was working for a leather tanner in Delaware—huh? Huh? That's not so great, and twenty-four isn't that much younger than me." I was seven. I sat in a canvas butterfly chair wearing a revolver and a Lone Ranger hat, but my father addressed me as if I were a professor from the university he'd never attended. "You know when Henry Ford's name first appeared in a paper?" he asked. "He was twenty, and a whirlwind blew him off a hayrick in Dearborn, Michigan. Hell, he was thirty-two before he even saw his first car—listen to this, Nugget (his nickname for me): 'I didn't often know if we'd have the rent,' Ford said of his early days. *But*, in the same breath, as if the incongruity had just hit him, he added, 'I just paid seventy-nine million dollars in taxes.' Imagine that!"

I was counting. "Twenty-six, twenty-seven, twenty-eight—"

My father chuckled, snapping his book closed. "You're gonna have a tough time getting to seventy-nine million that way."

"If he was twenty and you're thirty," I said, "then the difference is. . . ." I held all my fingers up in the air.

"No, no, no, that's not the point here." My father's hand closed over mine like a baseball glove over a couple of peas. "The point is that Henry wasn't anything at twenty. He didn't really get started *until* thirty-two, which puts me two years ahead." He showed me this number on his fingers. I flashed my ten back and he whipped his robe tail around the great hairy columns of his legs, looking wounded and betrayed.

～

It would have helped if my father had even been slightly aware of the efforts I was making to protect our family's reputation. In the fifth grade, I spent the entire semester explaining to my teacher, Mr. Franz, that my father traveled every weekend, to New Orleans, Salem, Asheville, Omaha, and thus would be unavailable, under any circumstances, to address our class about his profession, as everybody else's father did. However, Mr. Franz must have decided to go behind my back and call my father directly, because on the last Friday of the year, he stood up before the class and announced, "Today, children, we are going to hear from Jack's father, Mr. Alton Acheson, who has offered to lecture on the history of American business today."

My father's first rhetorical gesture had been to crack the cover of his favorite book, *A Railroad to the Sea*, and display the frontispiece photograph of Tom Durant, slouched in a coat with a mink collar thick as a tire tread and his hair grown long and curly past his ears. "Anybody in here recognize this guy?" he asked.

Preston Petersen had his hand up immediately and, with a sly look at the rest of the class, said, "Well, sir, he looks a lot like you."

My father gave a Bronx cheer. "I wish," he said. "Try again."

Others guessed the names of European kings or characters in Shakespeare—these being the only other men they'd ever heard of with long hair.

"Franz, you want a crack?" my father said, turning the photo to my teacher.

Mr. Franz must have guessed that this question was going to be coming around sooner or later and he tried to play along with it engagingly, polishing his glasses, put-

ting them back on again to squint. "Sorry, Mr. Acheson—stumped me."

"Nugget," my father said, turning to me. "Tell them who it is."

He had to wait for an answer until the class stopped breaking up at this introduction of my nickname. When they finally seemed to settle down, Preston shouted out, "Go on, answer him, Nugget!" breaking everybody up again.

"Never mind these morons," my father advised me from Mr. Franz's lectern. "They haven't been taught right. Just tell Franzy what you know."

Thanks to my father, I knew plenty about Tom Durant. I knew that he'd grown up in western Massachusetts. I knew he'd been a doctor. And I knew that around the time my father began studying Durant, he'd also stopped cutting his hair.

Instead, I made a face, widening my eyes and pulling my lips back in a grimace, begging my father to lecture about something else.

"*Please*, Nugget," someone said behind me.

"He was the president of the Union Pacific Railroad," I said resignedly. "He drove the golden spike, connecting the first train tracks across the country."

Once I got started it wasn't so bad. With my father's help (and hoping at the same time to distract attention from several cigarette burns I'd noticed in his lapel), I went over what he'd taught me of Durant's history: How he'd gotten hold of the Union Pacific in the first place by buying up all the stock under a false name, then electing himself treasurer. How Durant, needing a way to siphon off the money that Congress gave him, formed his own company to supply the railroad and then paid double or triple the actual cost to himself for the materials he might need, making sure that enough senators and congressmen had shares in the supply company. How Durant, knowing that he was getting paid per mile of laid track, had laid the tracks in a wiggle across Iowa to increase his pay. "This is the great tradition of American commerce, boys!" my father exclaimed in encouragement. "The question is, What do we do with it?"—statements that caused me to sink lower and lower in my seat. But not my father; he had points he wished to make. If this *was* the American way, then shouldn't it be taught practically? Why even mention the Transcontinental Railroad if students never learned Tom Durant's name? Or studied the brilliant methods he'd used to build his empire?

"I am sure, class," Mr. Franz said, hoarsely, "that Mr. Acheson is by no means trying to suggest that all American businesses are run this way."

"Only the ones that work," my father said. "The rest are just a dream."

After class, my father handed me a bulging manila folder of newsprint, its cover scribbled with the words "National Highway Defense Project." As usual, he was immune to the embarrassment of this. "So what do you think?" he asked, then added, "Before you answer, remember that Durant made his money by purchasing farmland out *ahead* of his railroad, then building tracks right through it, so the value went through the roof." We were walking then down the school's front drive, my classmates filing into their parents' Cadillacs and Packards on either side.

"Dad, I really don't think most of those guys were listening," I said.

"No, what do you think about my plan," my father said. He flipped through the newsprint in the folder, framed by shoe ads and women in slips, to one that proclaimed:

EISENHOWER ADOPTS FUNDING FOR INTERSTATE ROAD
Sends Bill to Congress

"See this, Nugget?" he said. "That's *my* railroad." But what I saw was the window of a Pierce-Arrow, filled with Preston Petersen's cross-eyed face.

One year later, my father put on his best pair of brushed oxfords and a panama hat and rode the streetcar to the Bowen Company offices on the Campanile. Prudential Bowen had turned seventy-five that year. His picture hung in every shop, Khrushchev-style, and banners fluttered with the legend *1882–1957, Thanks for 75 years of excellence, Mr. B!* Did my father see any danger in these things? If he did, he didn't show it as he marched straight past the secretary and down the long hall to the old man's office, where he tossed President Eisenhower's highway plan on his desk. "Sir," he said, "this road Ike's proposing is for real. National highway, coast to coast, Canada to Mexico. The ensuing demographic shift"—he stumbled, opening to a page not necessarily related to his comment—"is . . . well, it's a little bit ha-ha-hard to find. What troubles me, sir, is that no one at your company has so much as broken wind on how an interstate highway might affect real estate, which I happen to think is an important thing to know."

In the silence my father mouthed a cigarette with trembling fingers. Many a disgrun-

tled store owner, or competing developer, had sat here and cried, cajoled, and cursed the Bowen family, only to be met with the snowy crown of Prudential's head as he scratched away at his correspondence. But when my father burst out, "It's going to be the biggest land grab since Tom Durant stole half of Iowa for the Union Pacific, and I'd like to run it for you, please," the old man looked up, curiously.

"Do I know you?" he asked.

"I'm the messenger of destiny," my father said. He lit the cigarette.

The old man made a snorting noise, like a dolphin clearing its hole. He was also famous for having a live electric wire woven into the cushion of his visitor's chair that could be operated by a button under his desk, which was why my father put his briefcase down before he sat. "Why are you sitting on your briefcase, Acheson?" Prudential asked.

"Rumors, sir," my father said.

"Doesn't seem like much," the old man said. "Acting stupid on account of a rumor." As if by radio signal, his secretary slipped through the office door. "Get Livingston to check on this," Prudential told her, shoving the highway report her way, and then he returned to writing. For a time, my father just sat listening to the wet ruffle of the old man's breathing. There were complications here, ancient and dangerous reasons for mistrust—but my father shook them off. He stuck his hand out. "Give my best to Henry," he said. (This was the old man's son, whose office was two doors farther down the hall.) "And remember, it won't be a rumor when Ike sends the bulldozers in."

The next day my father made a lunch reservation at the Grotto Restaurant, downtown. I always liked going downtown better than going to the Campanile because when you crested Gillham Hill and first saw City Hall and the courthouse and the Warburton Building with their fire escapes etched against their sides, it felt like something was *coming up*. The trees dropped away and sunlight glared off the glass fronts of Western Auto,

Chapin Hardware, Sewall Wallpaper, and the newspaper building through whose barred windows the presses ran. And then finally, after waiting, you crossed Fourteenth Street and the sky darkened as the buildings closed in overhead, and the streetcar wires made a black net above the street, and the pigeons fluttered up from them. When I was a kid, the driver had let me hold the switch, the brass cool and wet beneath my fingers, but now I just watched, sitting beside my father, as the signs peeled out from the building fronts like flags for Gribble's and Kresge's and Emery, Byrd, Thayer's, for Baker's Qualicraft Shoes, and Rothschild's, founded in 1855.

The Grotto was at Twelfth and Baltimore. It had rows of red-checked tablecloths and brass-riveted booths under white trellises woven with plastic vines and a waitress came and led us to our seats. Usually the owner, Joey Ramola, escorted people in, and I could tell that my father didn't like being ignored by the way he lit his cigarette and blew his smoke toward the front of the restaurant, where Joey stood. We were also having lunch with my grandfather, Big Alton, a situation that frequently led to a blowup. I knew from experience that my father's blowups couldn't be prevented or hidden and so when I felt one coming on, I tried to concentrate on things I *could* control. I folded my napkin. I rearranged my silverware, my father's silverware, and my grandfather's silverware so that all the pieces were as close together as they could be without touching. As I bent down to sweep up a semicircle of crushed peanut shells from the floor, my father grabbed my arm. His touch was light, but his blue pupils looked fried. "Nugget," he said in a low voice, "I want to apologize to you ahead of time. The only way I could get your granddad to meet me was to bring you, too."

"All we're doing is having lunch, right?" I asked, hopefully.

"No," my father said. "No, I'm afraid it might be more important than that." Briefly, I saw his attention shift to the doorway, then back to me.

"Are we going to ask him for money?"

My father did, at least, grin at this. The one good thing about his blowups was that they were never directed at me. "Not this time," he said, adjusting my tie. "This time all we have to do is pretend that someone's giving us money."

"I don't see why *that* should be a problem."

"I hope it won't be," my father said. "But this is a very important deal for us, so right now, when your grandfather comes, I need you to promise me one thing."

"Don't worry about me, Dad," I said. "I know how to act." I'd stuffed the peanut shells in my pocket and was now dusting the pieces off my hands, but my father hooked his finger under my chin, so that I was forced to look up at him.

"Whatever happens," my father said, "just don't say anything."

My grandfather arrived in surprisingly good spirits. He had a bad knee, sometimes a war wound (he'd fought in 1918), others a riding injury. Unlike my father, he wore a gray English suit, shoulders square, and as he hobbled toward us across the restaurant, Joey Ramola scurried after him, shouting about the ponies—"Charolais, what a beauty!"—in his ear. When he sat down, he brushed off his coat sleeve where Ramola had touched him. "All I can tell you, Jack," he said, scooting in next to me, "is that I hope you never reach a point where it matters what a man like that has to say. The idea of a city coun-

cilman selling his independence for spaghetti on a plate. . . ."

Fortunately, it wasn't necessary to say much around my grandfather. He reeled off the names of politicians at the surrounding tables and then showed me the conditions under which an "elected official" could eat for a dollar—order placed between 1:30 and 1:45 on Tuesdays, Thursdays, and after 12:00 on Monday and Wednesdays, except bank holidays, choices only from the front side of the menu, no chipped beef, soup an extra $1.50 except when on special, no specials. This, my grandfather claimed, confirmed the corrupt nature of the place. I tried my best just to listen, though it didn't help to know that whatever blowup my father had planned would be witnessed by half the politicians in the city. My father did the same, avoiding the subjects that he and my grandfather normally argued about—except when the waiter came to take our order and my father, nodding at Big Alton, said, "He'll have the dollar spaghetti, I think." Toward the end of lunch, I saw my father check his watch, his gaze roving among the tables, and then he leaped up and collared a bandy-legged man in tortoise-shell glasses, wearing a suit the color of sand. "Colonel," he said brightly, pushing the man into our booth, "my father and I have agreed that you would be the perfect man to share our surprise."

"A surprise?" the colonel said. His mustache tips were the yellow of used cigarette filters and his eyes rolled soapily. "Alton, what's he talking about?"

"Whatever it is," my grandfather said, "I'm not involved."

My father, at that moment, lifted his leg and drove his heel so hard into Big Alton's knee that the breadbasket jumped. Or rather, this is what I believe must have happened. I saw only the sudden surge of blood to my father's cheeks, his tongue pressing the corner of his mustache, followed by a thump under the table and a gasp from my grandfather, who bent over beside me, his cheek white as his bread plate.

"I've instructed Pops not to comment," my father said.

"*That* seems irregular," the colonel said, trying to get up. "I think I'll—"

My father grabbed a half bottle of Chianti and three water glasses from an abandoned table, shoving the colonel fondly back in his seat.

"A toast," he said. "At least stay for that."

The colonel fingered his glass as if it were sticky.

"I'd still like to know what we're talking about," he said.

"*It's his birthday,*" my father whispered, and then stuck his thumb in his mouth, making a drinking motion. To my surprise, the colonel's face assumed a hooded look, and he chucked Big Alton's shoulder. "Alton, old man, congrats," he said.

I later learned that the whole conversation was a pretense, designed only for Tyler Livingston, whom Prudential Bowen had as-signed to read the highway plan. His starched white shirt and maroon-and-blue Bowen Company tie swept past us in the middle of our toast, ten minutes late for his usual table, but just in time to see what my father intended him to see: namely, himself and Colonel C.J. Pickering, a retired banker and possible investor, raising a glass of wine with conspiratorial smiles.

After this my father stood, reached across the table, and lifted me by my armpits over Big Alton's bent neck and onto the floor. "Gentlemen," he said, "there's nothing I'd rather do than stay around and talk shop, but I've got a streetcar to catch." And giving his father's shoulder a squeeze, he whispered, "Tell Joey to put it on my tab," and led me straight out of that place and back to the melting tar of Twelfth Street. ■

WHAT YOU MAY SEE ON SOME FINE DAY IN THE FUTURE.

PUTTING CREATIVITY TO WORK

by Catherine Liu

Aʜ, ᴄʀᴇᴀᴛɪᴠɪᴛʏ. We've always known it was desirable stuff, good for kids and poets and so on, but in the last few years creativity has entered that exalted realm of sacred social concepts. Today it ranks with "competitiveness" and "excellence" as one of the ineffable qualities that promises to make us all rich. Or maybe a little bit effable: Creativity, leaders and thinkers tell us, is essential for business, and as such it must be managed, protected, and actively promoted, not just left up to the haphazard experimentation of the "creatives" themselves. Indeed, from Taiwan to New Zealand, managers and policymakers are working to promote what they call "creative industries," which are supposed to rationalize the creative process and deliver earth-shaking creative leaps, all nicely wrapped and poised to boost tourism and puff stock markets and real estate prices onward into the skies.

In the U.K., which once considered "rebranding" itself as "Cool Britannia," the idea of creativity as a servant to business has guided government policy ever since New Labor came to power in 1997. Shortly thereafter, the Blair government established the Ministry of Culture, Media and Sport (the name itself is mind-boggling in its callow pragmatism), which was commissioned to promote such "creative industries" as fashion, advertising, architecture, TV, art, and what the ministry's website calls "interactive leisure software."

It did not take long for Pacific Rim countries to jump on Mother England's creativity bandwagon. In 2004, the newly re-elected center-right Australian government reaf-

firmed its commitment to supporting a "Digital Content Strategy" to promote people and businesses that produce "content," or what was formerly known as "culture." In Taiwan, where manufacturing is increasingly being off-shored to the People's Republic of China, the government has taken similar steps, launching a "Digital Content Institute" whose budget runs into the hundreds of mil-

lions of New Taiwan Dollars and whose website declares, matter-of-factly: "In this highly competitive information age, content rules."

As usual, though, it is the island nation of Singapore that is in hottest pursuit of today's trendy business idea. Singapore's plan is to make itself a "global arts city" by creating a more bohemian-friendly business environment where "creative workers" will want to live, play, and generate content. Even better, the city is called—optimistically—"Renaissance Singapore," according to a government report, a place where "building up a cultural and creative buzz" is an order from the highest authorities. You know the routine: Vibrancy. World-classness. Enthusiastic government support for the "scene." Even an annual gay festival, the largest in Asia—all in a country where anti-sodomy laws are still on the books. To announce its transformation from an over-sanitized corporate utopia to a cross between fifteenth century Florence and nineteenth century Paris, the Singapore government launched an advertising campaign on CNN International featuring a soulful writer-type testifying to his love of the magical richness of Singaporean cultural history and seductive textures of every day life in the creativity-friendly city-state. He is, of course, Irish.

It doesn't take a very creative sort to spot the irony here: Singapore may be infatuated with creativity these days, but it isn't a particularly democratic place. It is a "depoliticized" land that doesn't have much by way of opposition parties, and those who dare to stand against the ruling People's Action Party are frequently sued into bankruptcy under the country's stringent defamation laws. According to one highly regarded index of press freedom, Singapore earned by far the lowest ranking of all developed countries. In 2004, it found itself just one notch above Iraq and eighteen places ahead of Myanmar. (Singapore's response, according to the Associated Press: "Outsiders shouldn't equate freedom with criticizing the government.") Founded at the height of the Cold War, and in the wake of British attempts to put down Communists in Malaysia, the ruling People's Action Party has prided itself from the outset on its ability to maintain an orderly, spanking clean, multinational-friendly island of stability right on the equator. It set the gold standard for Asian modernization.

Those planning to take in the super-authentic street markets and ethnic festivals depicted in Singapore's ad campaign should know that its image heretofore has always been one of malls and chain stores; a place so bland that TGI Fridays was until recently considered an exciting place to cool one's heels on Saturday night. Indeed, Singapore is a kind of experiment in business rationality gone mad. Witness, for example, its infamous dabbling in social engineering: During

the sixties, Singapore's government grew concerned about the population boom and implemented a number of punitive policies to discourage large families, especially among the poor: These "population disincentives" included innovative features like preferred entry into elite primary schools for the children of parents who had agreed to be sterilized before the age of forty. By the beginning of the eighties, the opposite problem was threatening the island's stability: Now the government worried about the declining fertility of its upper classes. A government matchmaking agency was set up for yuppie lonely hearts too busy to date in order to encourage the "right" kind of procreative unions, with generous grants and, once again, preferred entry into elite public schools for the children of university-educated women.

Today it is creativity, not eugenics, that fires the fancy of Singapore's rulers. But the hyper-rational logic remains the same. The government still wants to engineer social progress and prosperity—only the new maxim is *art equals money*. The doctrine is spelled out with characteristic precision in a government paper titled "Culture and the Arts in Renaissance Singapore," in which it is calculated that art and cultural activities add value to a city at a greater rate of return ($1.66 on every dollar invested) than either the banking ($1.44) or petrochemical industries ($1.35). The strategy has two elements. First, the government hopes to encourage Singaporeans to be more creative themselves while at the same time creating a creativity-friendly environment in order to attract and retain creative foreigners. Naturally, Singapore calls these creativity-inducing measures "Art for Art's Sake" and "Art for Business' Sake." What one can be sure of, in the tightly controlled public sphere of the city-state, is that there will be little debate or creative dissent regarding these initiatives. Now that art has been declared good for business, the virtue of Singapore's progressive new cultural policies will have to become self-evident to its citizens.

Thus the winding path by which art for art's sake has become an official initiative of an authoritarian government. This may be extreme, but it should not be unfamiliar. After all, Singapore got the idea from us—specifically, from American theorists and American practices. For example, one of the island's "Renaissance" studies focuses on an American government report on the peculiar economics of Broadway theater, where experimentation has been stifled due to high production costs and the demands for immediate profitability. New plays and genuinely innovative drama must emerge from nonprofit theater. Conclusion of the American government: Nonprofit theater is an important contributor to theater profitability, and as such is a worthy recipient of government funding. Of course, when all theatrical productions are considered as potential profit-centers, any notion of "nonprofit" theater is rendered meaningless.

Once upon a time, of course, "art for art's sake" was a slogan accompanied by misery and poverty. It was a bohemian rejection of market values, not a rallying cry for the calculating social engineer. True, the suffering of the nineteenth-century bohemian was soon exploited in works such as Henri Murger's novel *Scenes of Bohemian Life* and Puccini's *La Bohème*, a favorite of every opera company's repertoire. Yet figures such as Manet, Baudelaire, and Flaubert made real material sacrifices in their attempts to achieve artistic autonomy. They were not team players. They cared little for the competitiveness of *la pa-*

trie. They favored mind-altering substances that would get them in deep, deep trouble in Singapore today. "Art for art's sake," in short, was a defiant refusal of the sort of values that are manifested today in desperate-to-be-hip chambers of commerce.

For modern-day economist Richard Florida, however, bohemians should be cele-

> **Art for art's sake has become an official initiative of an authoritarian government. This may be extreme, but it should not be unfamiliar. After all, Singapore got the idea from us.**

brated for their savvy cosmopolitan consumerism. Florida is a hip apologist for massive first world de-industrialization: he says he was motivated by growing up in the Rust Belt and watching the decimation of the blue-collar communities that nurtured him. His neoliberal solution for laid off industrial workers and their ruined cities? Get art! Be bohemian! Naturally Florida leaves out the downside of garret life—tuberculosis, drug addiction, prostitution or chronic un- and underemployment. What Florida affirms is the bohemian indifference to penny-pinching—their profligate, devil-may-care spirit (in Puccini's opera the bohemians spend their meager earnings in cafés and restaurants, on new clothes and jewelry, even though they can't pay their rent or medical bills). Bohemians like their amenities, he tells us: They dine out a lot, shop on credit, live beyond their means, and go to museums and theater. Bohemianism is a profit center, as well as a critical resource for city planners, a key to reinventing the urban landscape. Bohemians serve a debt-driven, service-oriented urbanity that closes the door on Protestant austerity and frugality. They drive up real estate values while fueling property speculation, as the skyrocketing condo prices of Brooklyn's

Williamsburg neighborhood seem to prove.

The court philosophers of this new creative empire have emerged from the academic left and cultural studies, from disciplines formerly given to proclaiming their hostility to the bourgeois way. These new-style pedagogues hack with confidence through the thicket of the old-school humanities, still inhabited by rare but dangerous "modernists" and "elitists," clear-cutting this once inhospitable terrain so that it can be made more useful to the creative-industrial state. Thus Terry Flew, one of the original administrators in the Creative Industries Faculty at Queensland University of Technology, proposes a "new humanism" in which "self-actualization" and "lifelong learning" would allow students to be, yes, "creative" and prepare for "everlasting uncertainty." Although Flew naturally dismisses the "old humanism" as an invention of the hated bourgeoisie, he seems to have no problem with market values themselves. The "new humanism" he describes is supposed to foster a better relationship between art and business, with business sifting cultural material like an eager Forty-niner panning for gold, and then offering in exchange the bright nugget of business-friendly ideology:

> [D]iscourses identified as having their origins in the arts have been filtered through to business and now returned to the artistic and cultural practice through the concept of the 'creative industries,' where artists are increasingly expected to view themselves as cultural entrepreneurs, managing creative talents, personal lives and professional identities in ways that maximize their capacity to achieve financial gain, personal satisfaction and have fun.

Because the workforce will have to face "everlasting uncertainty," the "new humanities" or "creative industries" are supposed to equip students for "lifelong learning." It is apparent that "everlasting uncertainty" is code for *no job security*, "lifelong learning" code for *constant retraining,* while "creativity" is code for *workforce docility*. The old humanism taught us to reform the system; the new version instructs us to reform ourselves, to become ready at any minute to be downsized

and "re-skilled." What the old humanism valued above all was democracy, but in the ideology of creative industry, democracy is what is most obviously missing, with its troublesome reverence for skepticism, dissent, debate, and critique. In Flew's benign account of business, each self-actualizing, creative person seems to exist all alone—actualizing, managing, adapting—so there is no need for dissent, dialogue, or politics at all.

It only gets worse. In a 2001 essay, "Creative Industries: From 'Blue Poles' to Fat Pipes," creative industries cheerleaders-in-chief Stuart Cunningham and John Hartley celebrate creative industries as "an idea whose time has come." Cunningham and Hartley begin by making fun of a painting that was and still is incomprehensible to most Australians: "Blue Poles" by Jackson Pollock, which was purchased by a Labor-led government in 1973 for a then-record price of $1.3 million. This is supposed to be high culture in all its absurdity. Ah, but "fat pipes"—these are the alternative to "Blue Poles": They are the healthy, pragmatic, non-elitist conduits by which the creative industries will irrigate the Australian cultural landscape. According to Cunningham and Hartley, creative industries are pretty special—they're sort of like Jesus. Not only will they make us rich (in spirit as well as bank account), but social hierarchy and prejudice will also fade into obsolescence once we "reconceptualize" creativity as industry. Before long, Cunningham and Hartley—in a routine tiresomely familiar to those of us who have to spend every day listening to cultural studies triumphalism—are mocking the effete "elitist" and celebrating the democratizing power of their new market-friendly university. "By bringing the arts into direct contact with large-scale industries such as media entertainment," they crow, "it allows us to get away from the elite/mass, art/entertainment, sponsored/commercial, high/trivial distinctions that bedevil thinking about creativity." They conclude that not only are arts and culture by nature elitist since they were once promoted by the aristocracy, but they are also coercive and punitive. Once they are supplanted by creative industries, however, we shall all be liberated from both ideology and history—and, it is to be presumed, from the dreaded penal system of culture itself.

So this is what freedom is to look like: "clustering, networking, R&D facilitation," and, of course, the promotion of the video game and movie industries—since, Hartley and Cunningham assert, these two sectors have been known to produce goods both "excellent" and "aesthetic." There will also be a great deal of marketing, plus the pursuit and identification of new markets to exploit. The plan for a creative-industries future looks a lot like, well, any other business plan, and it is just about as creative. Destroy the past and fuck tradition they tell us, but not in order to remake life in the image of art as the Dadaists proposed. Instead, we are to remake culture in the image of industry. At a time when university administrators have already sold off whole chunks of the academy to cor-

porations (medical schools at private and public universities from USC to the University of Minnesota have been sold to private health managers), Hartley and Cunningham are the first in line to implore their cult stud allies to sell off the humanities and arts education to business interests as well. Why? Because they suggest that humanities education that distances itself from free market directives is both oppressive and outdated. The irony, of course, is that elite universities and private liberal arts colleges are branding themselves with their superior brand of humanities education: market niche has become the goal for institutions of higher education. The sad thing is that for local, regional, and public institutions from the U.K. to Singapore to Australia and the U.S., "creative industries" will indeed fulfill some kind of vocational training function for its captive constituencies, contributing to the great and growing divide between the elites and those who will serve their interests—creatively. ■

THE FLIGHT OF THE CREATIVE CLASS
A BOHEMIAN RHAPSODY

By Paul Maliszewski and Thomas Frank

Dear Mayor Billings:

Provo needs a premier literary magazine.

In order to succeed in the twenty-first century and flourish economically, cities today must attract and retain the vital group of individuals that experts call "cultural creatives." Only by doing so can cities build a foundation for the high-tech industries and cutting-edge innovations that will dominate the future. A top-flight literary magazine is a vital part of that foundation—and the chance to get one to relocate to your area is a rare opportunity to guarantee robust growth.

I represent the editors and publisher of *The Baffler*, the award-winning literary magazine based in Chicago. For the past sixteen years, *The Baffler* has printed singularly invigorating takes on American business, economics, and history. Because of the skyrocketing costs of doing business in Chicago and an inept city government no longer attuned to their creative wavelength, *The Baffler* intends to move its offices, along with the entire *Baffler* team, to a metro area more interested in meeting creative people's needs.

In the highly influential and best-selling book *The Rise of the Creative Class*, Dr. Richard Florida rightly points out that cities have for too long focused on the wrong economic development goals. City officials have tried to attract and retain Fortune 500 corporations, but the cost of courting big businesses, as you well know, is steep. Besides, growth never comes. This is because, as Dr. Florida demonstrates, such cities have the picture upside-down. They were wooing the wrong people. Florida's groundbreaking discoveries make two things profoundly clear:

> *Creativity is the wellspring of competitive advantage,* and
> *Cities must attract creative people, as their creativity is important.*

Today's cutting-edge cities don't bother with big industrial corporations. Instead they are determined to attract highly talented, cutting-edge workers, men and women who design websites, develop new multivitamins and nutritional supplements, invent handy household devices, and dream up plans for fantastic machines like those robots with the arms, smart houses, jugs of milk that tell you when they're nearly empty, artificial brains, synthetic muscles and ligaments, and clothing with computers inside them. These creative individuals create growth through their boundless creativity. At heart, they are born entrepreneurs and natural self-promoters. When they band together, they make new companies, sharing ideas and combining them, synthesizing them more easily than generations past. And in the process, creative people create new job opportunities, by employing other people to work as their personal assistants, drivers, nannies, housekeepers, gardeners, and pool cleaners. Even better, major manufacturers and Fortune 500 companies are well known to move to areas where the creative work is already being done, to tap into its energy, capitalizing on it.

Creative people do have certain needs, however. They require hip entertainment, organic street-level culture, and artistic environments—from restaurants serving mind-boggling fusions of world cuisines, like Thai and Tex-Mex or Indian and Australian, to experimental theaters, avant-garde galleries, and authentic coffee shops with mismatched cups and saucers and deteriorating couches. Creative people crave lively street scenes and late-night music venues serving up pricey energy drinks in test tubes. In short, creative people insist they lead the sort of lives that feed their creativity, inspiring them. Luckily, cities today can provide those needs on a fairly modest budget. Supporting a literary magazine, after all, is much less costly than attracting a manufacturer of transmissions.

My clients, *The Baffler* team members, know the value of their creativity and have seen the phenomenal results firsthand. I invite you to read the enclosed literature, "The Baffler Miracle," an executive digest version of a feasibility report drafted by New Era. "The Baffler Miracle" will provide you with further details about how this exciting group of young people has worked their creative magic, and is ready to work it again, in their new home. I thank you for your time and look forward to speaking with you very soon about relocating *The Baffler* team to Provo.

Sincerely,

Edward Thomas

New Era Consultants ✳ *The* Relocation Specialists for the Creative Class

The Baffler Miracle

How a literary magazine transformed an American city

႘

In 1988, an editor, a historian, and a pre-med student met at the former sharecropper's cabin in Charlottesville, Virginia that they shared and discussed plans for their revolutionary publication, *The Baffler*. Acclaimed for their vision, these three creative individuals soon decided to partner with the city of Chicago, bringing their trademark blend of Southern gothic and Midwestern progressive literary traditions to the Land of Lincoln. That move proved fortuitous. When the Bafflers arrived, alternative rock blasting from their graffiti-covered cars, Chicago was gasping for its economic breath. It was a bleak relic of industrial America, a metropolis that just didn't get it. Blue-collar workers toiled in rusting steel mills and came home to decaying neighborhoods, burned-out schools, and dilapidated playgrounds. Executives commuted from the suburbs to jobs at dinosaurs like Sears and USX and always left the city before nightfall.

Today, Chicago is a vibrant and diverse market for talented people from around the globe, a textbook example of the power of creative communities to fuel economic development. Executives there long ago abandoned soulless commutes and have instead plugged themselves into the robust cultural potpourri that pours forth from cafés and corner theaters.

Chicago owes its newfound vigor to an authentic, street-level scene vibrant enough to capture the top position on national surveys of creative hot spots in each of the last six years. Creative enough to make the city a magnet for experimental poets, rule-defying chefs, and avant-garde musical outfits searching for a place to perform—and an audience to appreciate—their accomplished blends of hip hop, salsa, and zydeco. Unique enough to bring to Chicago a large population of entrepreneur-minded individuals who, as experts now understand, are the secret to economic success in our new age.

At the epicenter of this kaleidoscope of creativity stands a magazine, *The Baffler*, which has evolved from a spunky South Side startup to a nationally renowned cutting-edge content provider. In addition to re-launching Chicago as a literary hub, *The Baffler* has nursed the city's music scene, encouraging the work of pioneering drum-and-bass DJs and, at the magazine's many funky street festivals, bringing their infectious beats to thousands of fans. The Bafflers supplied a catalytic spark to the city's alt-radio community and remain staunch advocates of fusion cooking. From its headquarters in a battered brick structure that once served as a parking garage, *The Baffler* has become a symbol for the "zine" publishing revolution, an inspiration to thousands of poets, percussionists, and self-publishers hungry to join their zesty cultural movement.

Today the magazine serves as an incubator for local artists and entrepreneurs, sustaining their best work and focusing their collective efforts on dynamic economic growth. Some hold the magazine and its circle responsible for Chicago's dramatic rise up Dr. Richard Florida's Bohemian Index, a scientific ranking of the nation's most entrepreneurial zones. It's certainly easy to see why: original ideas and creative problem-solving are specialties of *The Baffler* staff.

And yet the Bafflers remain nonchalant about the changes they have wrought. At their office, revolutionary publications from around the world lie scattered amongst hand-me-down furniture, old concert posters, and brightly painted manikins (relics from a performance piece at last year's Freedom and Growth Festival). For all their awards, the magazine's creative leaders still blast alt-rock while driving around the city's South Side. And while they may sport a few more tattoos, they approach life with the same philosophy that propelled them so far: Let the creative flourish!

cs

Proven Leadership in Building Creative Communities

During its storied life *The Baffler* has generated economic growth in all the places it called home, ushering in new eras of prosperity as predictably as rainfall brings life to parched prairies. Other cities have built nightlife districts, started music festivals, and created other top-down entertainment opportunities. The facts show why they failed, and why only a *Baffler*-caliber magazine can attract creative individuals and insure unparalleled growth.

➢ The Woodlawn neighborhood of Chicago, where *The Baffler's* offices are located, has experienced total renewal since the staff moved in. A "no-go" area when they arrived, with unsafe streets, weed-strewn lots, and abandoned houses, Woodlawn is now home to a dazzling array of professors, visionaries and artist/facilitators. Those blocks of decaying tenements: gone. Rickety elevated railway: also gone. Attractive single-family homes: now available. What's more, real-estate prices are up, and experts predict a retail renaissance in the next three years.

➢ *Baffler*-sponsored readings at a Wicker Park coffee shop drew praise for their syncretic vision. While Wicker Park faced the familiar problems of urban blight, today it's an urban success story, recognized around the world for high-end art festivals, "indie" record labels, and dizzying growth in residential space boasting both black granite countertops and Sub-Zero refrigerators. MTV paid Wicker Park the ultimate compliment by setting the "Real World" there, and a major motion picture studio released a film named after the neighborhood.

➢ Chicago's a hot spot for talented, globally-minded nonconformists, making it a natural choice for corporate relocation officers. Aerospace giant Boeing, McGraw-Hill, UGN Inc., and Preferred Freezer have all moved there. The secret is out.

cs

Bohemias Don't Just Happen . . .

Bohemias are fragile ecosystems requiring complex planning, strategic partnering and, of course, incentivizing. Creative people like the Bafflers won't move to a city because they like the sound of its name; there must be a catalyst, a leader who assures them, *"Dude, this place rocks."*

The Bafflers stand ready to share their creative magic with another city. Whatever city the magazine adopts will see an immediate and substantial jump in Dr. Florida's Bohemian Index and enjoy the creative revitalization that Chicago experienced during what have come to be called its *Baffler* years.

Let Us Now Praise The Baffler

In 1985, when I moved to Chicago, it was all right. I mean, it was okay, but there was no nightlife apart from these neighborhood bars that had been there since like the 50s. Post-*Baffler*, I guess you could say, there's a lot more to do. People starting magazines, throwing parties, making music, having fun. Chicago's finally a great place to live.

Daniel Burdock, age 38
Account executive/tribal drummer

* * *

Do I agree with everything *The Baffler* writes? No, I do not. Do I respect *The Baffler*? I do. Look, a lot of the writing in there sounds like high-pitched whining to me, but I don't know, I'm not really the literary type or whatever. The thing is people read the thing, and they talk about it. And that's why I read it. It brings the city's young professionals together into a big conversation, like a town meeting except really cool. Now a lot of the people who read it, I don't like personally, but whatever. I still really respect how the magazine brings people together. That's powerful, and I must abide by that.

Alessandro Cortazar, age 24
Banker/home-brewer

* * *

After college, my parents told me I could move wherever I wanted to and they'd buy me an apartment so I could work on my films and live. I chose Chicago straightaway, without hardly even thinking about it. My older brother, Jason, went to Northwestern for journalism school and, one year, I was visiting him and he and his girlfriend at the time took me to one of the *Baffler*'s street festivals. It was so great. I think it was Rock Rock Weekend. Either that or Freedom and Growth, I can't remember now. I was seventeen or sixteen though, and I was like, "This is it, man. This is it!"

Ryan Holliwell, age 21
Independent Filmmaker

* * *

I met my last girlfriend reading *The Baffler*. We were both on the El, or I had just got on, and she was already there. Anyway, she was reading *The Baffler*, and I said to her, "Hey, new *Baffler*, where did you get that?" We struck up a conversation and talked the whole way. How cool is that? We were together six months, I think.

Melanie J. Blackman, age 30
Financial consultant/screenwriter

* * *

Lots of times my friends and I find out about some new fusion restaurant or a local gallery selling handicrafts by indigenous peoples from an advertisement in *The Baffler*. We think we've heard of every place. We've been to eat everywhere. We've done everything. But then a new issue will come and there will be all these ads for new places to go, and that's where we'll all go, to check them out for ourselves.

Peter Giullio, age 32
Lab technician/sci-fi author

* * *

A lot of editors and writers from *The Baffler* buy their used books from me or one of the other clerks. They also sell their review copies here. They're never in a rush. They're all pretty much approachable. I talk to them about books all the time. They're pretty smart. I told them to write more about the art world, but they haven't started doing that yet.

John Abol, age 19
Used bookstore employee/conceptual artist

Bafflomathy

Brian Chippendale spends his time half assing both his band, Lightning Bolt, and his art career. He lives in the increasingly gentrified city of Providence, Rhode Island, trying to hide the crumbly old mill he rents from the watchful eyes of speculative investors. *Ninja,* his book of comics and drawings, will be released by PictureBox Inc. in November 2006.

Steve Evans is an associate professor of English at the University of Maine. He tends a website about contemporary poetry at www.thirdfactory.net.

Thomas Geoghegan is a lawyer in Chicago and has written several books, including *Which Side Are You On?* and *The Secret Lives of Citizens.*

Catherine Liu teaches at the University of California at Irvine. She is the author of a novel, *Oriental Girls Desire Romance,* and an academic monograph, *Copying Machines: Taking Notes for the Automaton.* She is at work on a book about academic populism, critical theory and astrology.

Jim McNeill is a labor bureaucrat in Washington, D.C. He was editor of *The Racine Labor* and managing editor of *In These Times.* His writing has appeared in the *American Prospect,* the *Chicago Tribune* and *Dissent.*

Andrew O'Hagan's most recent novel is *Personality.* It won the James Tait Black Memorial Prize and the E.M. Forster Award from the American Academy of Arts and Letters. He is a contributing editor to the *London Review of Books.*

Jena Osman's most recent book is *An Essay in Asterisks* (Roof 2004). She teaches in the graduate creative writing program at Temple University.

Kim Phillips-Fein is an assistant professor teaching American history at New York University. Her first book, about the role of business in the rise of conservative politics, is forthcoming from Norton. She is getting married this fall, 'cause she knows when to hold 'em.

Martin Riker lives in Denver. He is currently working on a book about composer and instrument inventor Peter Smith.

Joshua Schuster has poetry published by Handwritten Press and has essays in *Open Letter* and *Other Voices.* He is a graduate student at University of Pennsylvania.

Whitney Terrell is the author of *The King of Kings County* and *The Huntsman.* He's the New Letters Writer in Residence at the University of Missouri-Kansas City and remains, absurdly, a Royals fan.

Matt Weiland is from Minnesota, Michigan, Iowa, and Ohio. He is co-editor of *The Thinking Fan's Guide to the World Cup,* published by Harper Perennial. He lives in London, where he is the deputy editor of *Granta.*

Geoffrey Young's latest book is *Fickle Sonnets.* He runs the Geoffrey Young Gallery in Great Barrington, Massachusetts.